Adhd for Women

A New Approach to Understanding and Curing
Your Adhd

(Teaching the Basics of Social Skills to Improve
Emotional Intelligence)

Gerald French

Published by Rob Miles

© **Gerald French**

All Rights Reserved

ISBN 978-1-990084-22-5

Legal & Disclaimer

The information contained in this book is not designed to replace or take the place of any form of medicine or professional medical advice. The information in this book has been provided for educational and entertainment purposes only.

The information contained in this book has been compiled from sources deemed reliable, and it is accurate to the best of the Author's knowledge; however, the Author cannot guarantee its accuracy and validity and cannot be held liable for any errors or omissions. Changes are periodically made to this book. You must consult your doctor or get professional medical advice before using any of the suggested remedies, techniques, or information in this book.

Table of Contents

Introduction

The impression of attention deficit hyperactivity disorder (ADHD) depends on the existence of an adequate number of signs of abnormally large amounts of impulsivity, hyperactivity, and heedlessness that have been existing since early adolescence and are keeping with the individual's formative age and that happen in more than one setting (for instance, at home and in school). All youngsters, to some degree, demonstrate behaviors of absentmindedness, hyperactivity, and impulsivity at different times and these behaviors are known to be impacted by framework of reference.

A finding lays on clinical judgment utilizing institutionalized criteria, at times with the help of parental and instructor questionnaires. Expanding rates of diagnosis, rising utilization of stimulants, absence of proof for long haul viability for stimulants, pharmaceutical advertising practices, and absence of confirmation for an identifiable hidden neurological issue, have all added to contention encompassing the diagnosis.

ADHD is a term that gives a depiction to an arrangement of behaviors, yet does not give a clarification; it does not reveal the reason for these behaviors. A finding alone accordingly cannot let us know what medications may be most useful for any individual kid and their family. Moreover, despite the fact that stimulants enhance behaviors in the short-term results following lengthy treatment discovers minimal significant contrasts between the individuals who did or did not get pharmacological treatment, indicating the significance of non-pharmaceutical based methodologies.

Chapter 1: What Are The Signs And Symptoms Of Adhd?

The diagnosis of ADHD must be based from a compilation of sources including observation, behavioral history, medical exams, and a psychological examination by a qualified psychologist. The behavioral studies must also be assessed in multiple environments. The reason for this, if a person is hyperactive or impulsive at school, but exhibits normal behaviors at home, then ADHD may not be the cause, yet other factors such as bullying or other issues resulting in the behavior. A comprehensive neuropsychological evaluation should be performed to ensure that the behavior is not a result of other psychological conditions, or other conditions such as a learning disorder or language disorder that may be assumed as being ADHD. Other areas that need to be assessed is the home environment. This can be assessed by isolating the child from the parents in a calm setting and asking specific questions, on level for the age of the child, so they feel comfortable answering them. Abused and/or neglected children will tend to appear inattentive, have lack of focus, and depressed. They will seem uninterested in activities, and will appear to be in another world. This can also be miss-diagnosed as ADHD.

ADHD is thought to be centered on the development of the frontal lobe region of the brain. While the frontal lobe of humans is not fully developed until about the age of twenty, initial signs of ADHD can be seen in very young children. ADHD behavior usually become apparent when a child is around 4 years of age. It is recommended however, the diagnosis of ADHD should not be made in a child younger than 4 years old. Teachers tend to also be the first to identify there is an issue with a child. The reason for this is they have an immediate comparison tool with them, other children. It can be easy to spot a potential problem when a child is acting differently than other children of same age and development. Teachers should be taught on how to identify the early signs of mental disorders so they can convey the concerns to the parents. Some indicators that teachers should look out for are, children that require a significant amount of time to complete tasks, making numerous careless mistakes, frequently interrupt the teacher, not remaining seated when told to do so, or constant talking or chatter when told not to. Early detection is key to getting the correct treatment options in place so the child has a much better chance at success.

Hyperactive or impulsive behaviors, which tend to be noticed first, include fidgeting, squirming about, the inability to sit still, aggression towards peers (hitting, kicking, biting), excessive energy, verbal or physical outbursts, impatience, constant talking, and constantly interrupting others. These inattentive behaviors often become noticeable once when a child enters school. He or she might be easily distracted, have difficulties in following instructions, be forgetful, struggle with tasks, and generally appear unaware to what's going on around them.

Boys are typically diagnosed with ADHD more than girls. The main thought behind this is because girls tend to experience the disorder differently. Children with a close biological relatives, with ADHD, are more likely to be affected with ADHD themselves.

ADHD in teenage children can be more challenging as they progress into the higher grade levels in school, instead of being with the same teacher and students all day, they are faced with multiple teachers and different students. The added schedules of different class locations, additional homework and a more challenging curriculum, can be overwhelming to ADHD suffers. If children are not diagnosed with ADHD during their elementary years, it becomes more difficult to be identified in adolescent years. Teachers now have less time with each child and they might not pick up on the signs and symptoms. Parents should make sure they keep on top of what their children are learning and keep watch for some of the same symptoms as younger children. One of the main differences is that older children will sometimes lose the hyperactivity side of ADHD and become more of the Inattentive type.

Signs and Symptoms of hyperactive or impulsive ADHD

Fidgeting, squirming or trouble staying in one place or waiting his turn

Excessive running, climbing or being destructive

Trouble playing quietly, even when alone

Extreme impatience, wanting things right now

Always seems to be "on the go", constantly moving about, almost as if they had a motor running full speed inside them

Excessive talking, interrupting or blurting out answers

Signs and Symptoms of Inattentive ADHD

Makes careless decisions

Is easily distracted

Has difficulty adhering to or following instructions

Doesn't seem to be listening when directly spoken to

Has trouble being organized

Avoids or dislikes working on things in a sustained way

Is quite forgetful, always losing things

Chapter 2: An Illness Or Simply A Phase?

Whenever you were a child, didn't you play around continuously without a particular purpose? Didn't you continuously turn your concentration on one factor to another? Didn't you have a problem sitting still? Didn't you have a hard time focusing on a single matter, for an extensive length of time? You were a child and you socialized the way almost all children do. You didn't reflect about things, you just did them since at this age, there is no thinking process. Almost all children cope with this stage within their beginning life, however technology moved forward as well as informed you that perhaps this process is not so common.

ADHD, how may we explain it? You would think with all the great minds in the world that an individual may have produced an profile that fits. But that's not the problem - it appears that ADD is certainly a random definition rather than essentially an illness.

There's still puzzlement over who might or might possibly not have ADD. A few affiliates in the mental health association stood a demand to classify anybody with ADD, as obtaining a brain deficiency. Apparently it had been for that reason that the initial quantity of ADD patients that have been examined happen to be ill with encephalitis, that's a degeneration in the brain. However, this qualifying requirement isn't valid any longer, because over time, people without any brain insufficiencies, are actually put in the roll of ADD.

At this time around, you'll find two most critical kinds of ADD. ADD with attention deficit hyperactivity disorder and ADD without attention deficit hyperactivity disorder. Indications of ADD plus attention deficit hyperactivity disorder are known to as: can't continue sitting, restless, increases or runs a good deal, talks much, can't play silently in addition to getting in trouble standing in line or waiting for their turn. A few indications of ADD without attention deficit hyperactivity disorder are, disordered, getting in trouble concentrating on tasks, with no trouble getting diverted and does not appear to provide consideration.

Therefore, is that ADD? The amounts generally given are three to five percent of those. But nobody knows. Since ADD is really arbitrary, it's apparent that several who're listed as ADD, might not even easily fit in there.

There's still an essential debate happening regarding the validness of ADD. Could it be genuine? Numerous people state that ADD isn't a disease, however a selection of actions and signs, that could often be produced by a variety of troubles. So when you include the matter that the specialists within the area, can't even come to a decision on which precisely ADD is and who precisely has it, this only gives more credibility to individuals that gave a suspicion over the existence of ADD. Obviously you will find many individuals who take into account that ADD is reputable and not simply some stage one is dealing with. They take into account that people needs to be taken proper care of for his or her signs and symptoms and never be likely to simply get free from them.

Chapter 3: What Is Attention Deficit (Hyperactivity) Disorder?

ADD is the general term used to describe people with ADHD. Both terms pretty much mean the same thing, however there are three types of ADHD. These include the Inattentive Type, the Hyperactive-Impulsive Type and the Combined Type.

The disorder is a genetic neurobehavioral problem that is most common among children, but also affects adults. Basically, our nerve cells or neurons send chemical messengers back and forth called neurotransmitters. These messengers are what tell our bodies how to think, how to act and how to feel. Some research studies claim that ADHD is a genetic deficiency of these chemical messengers and they are not communicating like they should.

What Causes ADHD?

One of the causes for ADHD stems from problems in the gut (digestive issues) and food allergies or sensitivities. NourishedHealth.com has a fantastic article talking about the ADHD and food – specifically gluten and caesin sensitivities as a cause to ADHD. I highly suggest you give it a read.

ADHD is still being studied extensively and scientists really aren't sure yet what **exactly** causes it. However, they have found that hormones also play a role.

Recent studies show that the brain chemical, dopamine, may play a role in ADHD. Dopamine is an important chemical that carries signals between nerves in the brain. It is linked to many functions, including movement, sleep, mood, attention, and learning. – Web MD

Also, Norepinephrine, a stress hormone, is known to affect the parts of the brain where attention and response actions are controlled. We do know that increasing the levels of dopamine and norepinephrine in the brain have helped with ADHD symptoms.

Symptoms of ADHD

The list below outlines the symptoms of these three types of ADHD.

Symptoms of *inattention*:

Easily distracted

Bored with a task after only a few minutes, unless they are doing something enjoyable

Often lose things

Don't seem to listen when spoken to

Easily confused

Difficulty processing information as quickly and accurately as others

Struggle to follow instructions

Symptoms of *hyperactivity*:

Fidgety and squirmy

Talk nonstop

Trouble sitting still

Difficulty doing quiet tasks or activities

Symptoms of *impulsiveness*:

Impatience

Inappropriate comments

Show emotions without restraint

Act without thinking about consequences

Interrupt others

source: National Institute of Mental Health (NIMH)

All of us experience these symptoms once in a while. But, someone experiencing true symptoms of ADHD will be struggling with these issues more often than not. Some people may think their child has ADHD when in fact it's simply misbehavior.

Follow the natural methods mentioned below for overcoming ADHD (for adults and children).

Create a Routine

Children with ADHD are drawn to new activities, adventure, and change. Yet they're balanced by the opposite: activities that are calming, relaxing, and nurturing. Your son needs regularity and structure to counter his natural tendency toward chaos: a regular time to do his homework, exercise, relax, eat, go to bed, and wake up to begin a new day. Here's some advice about how to create a vata-calming environment for him at home.

Relaxation

Do a 5- to 10-minute relaxation with your son at least once a day. Lie down on the floor or in bed in shavasana (corpse pose), supporting your heads with a pillow and covering up with a blanket to stay warm. Then ask your child to feel his body from head to toe. Turn the practice into a game; together, pretend you are a scoop of ice cream melting in the sun, or that you're sinking into a huge feather pillow. Imagine your breath is like the waves of the ocean— or ask your child to instruct you. The idea is to get your child to relax and deepen his breath, which helps his CNS switch from a sympathetic mode, which is a "fight-or-flight" state, to a parasympathetic mode, which is a nourishing and restorative state. Try this when your child comes home from school, or before supper or bedtime; these are times when our kids can be most overstimulated.

Bedtime Massage

Oil is the quintessential vata balancer, so a bedtime massage is particularly calming for children with ADHD. To begin, wet your hands and pour a teaspoon of organic unrefined oil in your palm. (Olive, almond, and sesame oils are especially grounding.) Then rub your hands together and massage the mixture into your child's skin. Let the oil soak in for a few minutes, then towel off any remaining residue. Try to do this at least once a week. If you don't have time to give your child a head-to-toe treatment, just massage his feet (covering them with socks to protect the sheets). If your child has trouble falling asleep, this bedtime activity will help.

Diet and Nutrition

Despite multiple studies in the last 20 years suggesting that diet and food additives can exacerbate hyperactivity, the current medical stance is that there is no causal link between food and ADHD. In my own practice, parents who have reduced their child's intake of sugar, refined foods, and foods with chemical additives (food dyes, preservatives, MSG, etc.) report significant improvement in their child's behavior over four to eight weeks. These children are also less disruptive and more focused when they eat plenty of cooked vegetables and whole grains, along with moderate amounts of protein and organic unrefined oils.

In addition, give your son 50 mg of B-complex vitamins and 100 to 200 mg of fish oils geared for children. These supplements nourish and stabilize the CNS while improving mood stability, mental focus, and brain function.

Natural Rx

Herbs that calm, soothe, and nourish the nervous system include lemon balm, chamomile, hops, passion flower, skullcap, brahmi, valerian, and St. John's Wort. They can be taken safely as teas or tinctures—just follow the instructions on the bottle or box. (Dosing for children is one-fourth to one-half the adult dose based on their weight.)

Technology Time-Out

Most of our kids are perpetually plugged in—texting on their cell phones, playing computer games, watching TV for hours on end. This constant electronic stimulation not only fragments their attention but also exposes them to electromagnetic radiation (EMR) at potentially harmful levels. When a child is sensitive, this exposure agitates his nervous system. Sleep disturbances, chronic fatigue, headaches, dizziness, memory and attention problems, and distorted vision are all possible side effects of EMR. Try to limit how much electromagnetic exposure your child is getting by reducing his screen time to an hour or less a day.

Minimal Medication

If you decide to give your child medication, find a doctor who is willing to work with you to find the minimal dose that is effective. Ask your doctor to allow your child to take "holidays" from the medication when intense concentration and focus aren't necessary (on the weekends, during summer break, etc.). By carefully monitoring your child's behavior, you can help your doctor find the dosage and schedule that allow him to succeed in school, while decreasing his chances of experiencing side effects.

Forgo Food Colorings and Preservatives

Alternative treatments may help manage some symptoms associated with ADHD, including:

difficulty paying attention

organizational problems

forgetfulness

frequently interrupting

The Mayo Clinic notes that certain food colorings and preservatives may increase hyperactive behavior in some children. Avoid foods with these colorings and preservatives:

sodium benzoate

FD&C Yellow No. 6 (sunset yellow)

D&C Yellow No. 10 (quinoline yellow)

FD&C Yellow No. 5 (tartrazine)

FD&C Red No. 40 (allura red)

Avoid Potential Allergens

Diets that restrict possible allergens may help improve behavior in some children with ADHD.

It's best to check with an allergy doctor if you suspect your child has allergies. But you can experiment by avoiding these foods:

chemical additives/preservatives like BHT and BHA

milk and eggs

chocolate

foods containing "salicylates" like berries, chili powder, apples and cider, grapes, oranges, peaches, plums, prunes, and tomatoes

Try EEG Biofeedback

Electroencephalographic (EEG) biofeedback is a type of neurotherapy that measures brain waves. A 2011 study suggested that EEG training was a promising treatment for ADHD.

A child may play a special video game during a typical session. They'll be given a task to concentrate on, such as "keep the plane flying." The plane will start to dive or the screen will go dark if they're distracted. The game teaches the child new focusing techniques over time. Eventually, the child will begin to identify and correct their symptoms.

Get (or Give) a Massage

Massage is relaxing. But it may be more than that for those with ADHD. A 2003 study published in the journal **Adolescence** examined the effects of massage on mood and behavior. Students with ADHD who received massage therapy for 20 minutes twice a week over the course of a month experienced improved mood in the short term and improved classroom behavior in the longer term.

Chapter 4: What Is Adhd? Definition & Meaning

Attention deficit hyperactivity disorder (ADHD or ADD) is a complex brain disorder that impacts approximately 11 percent of children aged 4-17 and almost 5 percent of adults in the United States. ADHD is not a behavior disorder. It is a developmental impairment of the brain's self-management system and executive functions.

"ADHD is not a breakdown of the brain in one spot. It's a breakdown in the connectivity, the communication networks, and an immaturity in these networks," says Joel Nigg, Ph.D., professor of psychiatry at Oregon Health & Science University. "These brain networks are interrelated around emotion, attention, behavior, and arousal. People with ADHD have trouble with global self-regulation, not just regulation of attention, which is why there are attentional and emotional issues.

What Are the 3 Types of ADHD

There are three distinct subtypes of ADHD:

• Hyperactive-Impulsive ADHD

• Inattentive ADHD (formerly called ADD)

• Combined ADHD

People with hyperactive-impulsive ADHD act "as if driven by a motor" with little impulse control — moving, squirming impatiently, and interrupting others. People with inattentive ADHD are easily distracted and forgetful. They may be daydreamers who lose track of homework, cell phones, and conversations with regularity.

What Are the Symptoms of ADHD

Common symptoms of ADHD include inattention, lack of focus, poor time management, weak impulse control, exaggerated emotions, hyper focus, hyperactivity, and executive dysfunction.

Doctors diagnose ADHD using symptom criteria from the (DSM-V), which lists nine symptoms that suggest Inattentive ADHD and nine that suggest Hyperactive-Impulsive ADHD. A child may be diagnosed with ADHD only if he or she exhibits at least six of nine symptoms from the ADHD symptoms and if the symptoms have been noticeable for at least six months in two or more settings for example, at home and at school. What's more, the symptoms must interfere with the child's functioning or development, and at least some of the symptoms must have been apparent before age 12. Older teens and adults may need to consistently demonstrate just five of these symptoms in multiple settings.

ADHD Symptoms in Children

Common Symptoms of Hyperactive-Impulsive ADHD in Children

- Talks excessively and blurts out answers
- Acts as if "driven by a motor"
- Fidgets and squirms in seat constantly

Common Symptoms of Inattentive ADHD in Children

- Distracted or short attention span
- Struggles to organize tasks and activities
- Often loses things and is forgetful

ADHD Symptoms in Adults

Roughly two-thirds of people who experienced ADHD symptoms as a child will continue to experience ADHD symptoms as an adult, though its manifestations change with age.4 What's more, many people with attention deficit were undiagnosed or misdiagnosed as children. They may suffer serious psychological consequences after a lifetime of blaming themselves for ADHD symptoms such as:

• Forgetting names and dates

• Missing deadlines and leaving projects unfinished

• Extreme emotionality and rejection sensitivity

•Becoming easily distracted and disorganized

• Suffering anxiety and depression

What Causes ADHD

ADHD a brain-based, biological disorder. It is not caused by bad parenting, too much sugar, or too many video games. Scientists are investigating whether certain genes, especially ones linked to the neurotransmitter dopamine, play a role in developing ADHD.5 Additional research suggests that exposure to toxins and chemicals may increase a child's risk of having ADHD.

ADHD Diagnosis Information

Any good ADHD diagnosis is based on the criteria defined in the DSM-V. A clinical interview is performed to gather the patient's medical history, and is often supplemented with neuropsychological ADHD tests, which offer greater insight into strengths and weaknesses, and helps identify co morbid (or co-existing) conditions. It can take several hours of talking, test taking, and analysis by an ADHD specialist to diagnose symptoms.

How Is ADHD Diagnosed

Though your child may have some symptoms that seem like ADHD, it might be something else. That's why you need a doctor to check it out.

There is no specific or definitive test for ADHD. Instead, diagnosing is a process that takes several steps and involves gathering a lot of information from multiple sources. You, your child, your child's school, and other caregivers should be involved in assessing your child's behavior. A doctor will also ask what symptoms your child has, how long ago those symptoms started, and how the behavior affects your child and the rest of your family. Doctors diagnose ADHD in children after a child has shown six or more specific symptoms of inattention or hyperactivity on a regular basis for more than 6 months in at least two settings. The doctor will consider how a child's behavior compares with that of other children the same age.

Your child's primary care doctor can determine whether your child has ADHD using standard guidelines developed by the American Academy of Pediatrics, which says the condition may be diagnosed in children ages 4 to 18. Symptoms, though, must begin by age 12.

It is very difficult to diagnose ADHD in children younger than 5. That's because many preschool children have some of the symptoms seen in ADHD in various situations. Also, children change very rapidly during the preschool years.

In some cases, behavior that looks like ADHD might be caused instead by:

A sudden life change (such asdivorce, a death in the family, or moving)

Undetected seizures

Medical disorders affecting brain function

Anxiety

Depression

Bipolar disorder

ADHD Treatment Options

The best ADHD treatment strategies are multimodal ones — combinations of several different, complementary approaches that work together to reduce symptoms. Most ADHD treatment plans include one or more of the following:

ADHD medication including a stimulant like Adderall (amphetamine) or Ritalin (methylphenidate), or a non-stimulant like Strattera or Intuniv

An ADHD diet low in sugar and carbohydrates, and high in protein, greens, and omega-3 fatty acids

ADHD vitamins and supplements particularly zinc, iron, Vitamin C, Vitamin B, and magnesium, which are critical to healthy brain function.

Behavioral Therapy for ADHD, which works best in improving ADHD-associated oppositional behaviors in children, as well as other areas of functioning, like interactions with parents and school, when combined with medication.

ADHD therapies that run the gamut from cognitive behavioral therapy (CBT) and occupational therapy to art or music therapy to play therapy and beyond

Natural remedies for ADHD like mindfulness meditation, brain training, or exercise

How to Find ADHD Doctors

"ADHD is generally ignored in medical education," says William Dodson, M.D., an ADHD specialist and author. "Just 5 years ago, 93 percent of adult psychiatry residencies didn't mention ADHD in four years of training and, amazingly, half of pediatric residencies didn't mention ADHD."

Finding a medical professional who understands ADHD and its comorbid conditions is not easy, but it is vital if you hope to secure an accurate diagnosis and proactive treatment plan. Use these criteria to find an ADHD doctor or other specialist near you.

Can what you eat help attention, focus, or hyperactivity? There's no clear scientific evidence that ADHD is caused by diet or nutritional problems. But certain foods may play at least some role in affecting symptoms in a small group of people, research suggests.

Chapter 5: What Is Adhd

Attention deficit hyperactivity disorder that is connoted with ADHD is known to be a medical condition associated with the development of the brain and its activity that affects the following:

It affects attention

Sitting still

It affects self-control

This medical condition do affects a child or children in the following ways: It can affects among friends

If can affect at home

Even at school

This medical condition affects children of school age and can also affect them till adulthood. This medical condition is usually most commonly diagnosed mental disorder in teens and it affects them to the extent that they will not be able to get their impulses controlled or possibly have problems with paying attention which has a serious and life threatened effects at home and even in school. This medical condition is more in male child than the female ones.

Grown up child with ADHD have the following problems: They have problem in time management

They have organizational problems

They have issues with goal settings

They do not get job easily

They have issues or problems in any relationship they found themselves

They are addicted

No positive self esteem

SIGNS AND SYMPTOMS OF ADHD

They are basically of three categories, they are:

Category A (inattention)

A child with ADHD often lose off things

Daydream problems

Such children do not sit to do things

Do not have ability to organize things

They are too forgetful

They make careless mistakes

They do not pay attention

They do not have a listening ear

They do not end projects well

They have no direction

Gets distracted easily

Category B (Hyperactivity)

Such in this category assumes a drive, i.e. being forced

Talks much

In this category, such children are restless

They do not play quietly

They move about

Such children in this class usually bounce when seated

Category C (Impulsivity)

Such in this category do not wait for turn

Gives answers out easily

Disturbs others

ADULT SYMPTOMS OF ADHD

It's good to know that as this medical condition grows to

adulthood, symptoms also changes, signs like;

Fatigue

Postponing   thing

Lateness

Being   forgetful

Under   rating   oneself

Do not have the ability to control his or her   anger

Brings   himself   or   herself   down

Such do have problems at work They are usually   addicted

Impulsiveness

They   are   not   organized

They   get   frustrated   easily

Depression

They   lack   concentration

Their   mood   gets   swings   with   time

Issues in relationship cannot be written off

ADHD   DIAGNOSIS

This medical condition is usually diagnose or   evaluated

comprehensively by a licensed clinician like: A   psychologist

A   pediatrician

Psychiatrist who has a deep knowledge in ADHD.

Whoever wanted diagnosing ADHD will ensure that the seen or known symptoms are not as a result of any medical conditions such as mental disorder or condition.

Children with this medical condition are usually diagnose during early school age, an adult with ADHD diagnosis, it really means that such a child has had this medical condition before he or she grew up to a certain age.

This medical condition do show up when one is usually between the age of 3-6 years and it can continue till one grows up, Mistakes should not be made when a child is down emotionally or possibly has disciplinary problems, or when a child is so quiet. If this medical condition is not diagnosed in adult, the followings are it effects:

Failed affairs

Poor relationships

Issues at work

Poor performance to work

This medical condition changes with time as one grows older, in children, these two are mostly predominant

Hyperactivity Impulsivity

But, as time grows on and as he or she gets to a higher stage of learning, INATTENTION may set in which will be the cause of the child's poor performance.

Adults with this medical condition struggle with the following behaviors:

Relationship problems

They are usually restless

They are usually not at rest and paying attention to

They are not usually socially active.

The stage of impulsiveness usually persists till they grow up.

Chapter 6: Add And Adhd Explained

Attention deficit disorder (ADD) and attention deficit hyperactivity disorder (ADHD) are interchangeable terms for a psychological ailment that afflicts some 5.9 million children in the United States, and millions of children around the world. But these are not limited to children alone. Although it may show its first symptoms during childhood, ADD and ADHD also afflicts millions of adults worldwide. There just happens to be more active monitoring of the ailment and other psychological disorders in the US, and that's why there is more data and statistics about the disorder available in American publications and online resources.

What is ADD and ADHD?

The terms ADD and ADHD were not in use until 1980, although the ailment has been recorded in medical journals since the later 1700s. The ailment was first clearly described in 1902, but the terminology in use included "mental restlessness," "minimal brain dysfunction," "hyperkinetic reaction of childhood," and "attention deficit disorder" in 1980. This is documented in the Diagnostic and Statistical Manual (DSM) of mental disorders. Now, ADD is used to describe that condition in which the patient exhibits symptoms of inattentiveness and lack of focus and interest, while ADHD refers more to the hyperactivity side of the ailment. These references describe one common psychiatric ailment where the visible symptoms are problems of attention, hyperactivity, or impulsive behavior that may not be appropriate for a person's age.

There is no known cause of ADHD, but there are three factors related to its occurrence – heredity or genetics, a neurobiological disorder in the brain, and environmental influences. As for genetics, studies indicate that the disorder can be inherited from parents, and that siblings of children with ADHD have a bigger change of developing the same. When environmental factors are considered, alcohol consumption during pregnancy could cause a fetal disorder the symptoms of which can be similar to those of ADHD. Exposure to toxic substances like lead or polychlorinated biphenyls and some organo-phospate insecticides can also increase the risk developing ADHD, but inconclusive as to being the actual cause.

The neurobiological disorder factor in ADHD is caused by a chemical imbalance in the brain which affects neurotransmission, which simply put is the transmission of messages by means of neurons within the brain cells that result into action or inaction on the part of the individual. Sometimes there are disproportionate amount of neurotransmitter chemicals that result either in inattentiveness, or hyperactivity.

Traumatic brain injury during childhood could be a likely factor, since about 30% of those injured have been found to have developed ADHD. There were also a small number of cases that have been attributed to a previous infection or trauma to the brain.

Chapter 7: The Journey Begins

Although medication coupled with professional help can play a large part in your child's life, what he needs most of all are parents that care for him and champion his needs. Just as for any other child, it is the parent who will build his character, who will teach him right from wrong and prepare him for the rest of his life.

Despite your personal situation, once your child has been diagnosed with ADHD there are some steps that you should take. First, you should make sure you understand what your child's condition really is. If you are not fully confident of your doctor's ability to make such a diagnosis then by all means get a second opinion. There should be a psychological as well as a medical evaluation done so more than one medical professional should be involved.

Research and training

Once you have accepted the diagnosis, learn all you can about the disorder. It's important to learn as much as possible about the causes of the disorder as well because parents have a tendency to blame themselves whenever their children are found to have special needs. The more information you have on the causes of ADHD, the less likely you are to feel guilty about your child being diagnosed with it. You must acknowledge that you are not to be blame for your child's disorder even if other people try to make you think that you are. Ignorant people often feel that when a child with ADHD has a tantrum or behaves badly in a public place it is simply the result of poor parenting. Remember always that ADHD is a brain disorder and so not the result of anything that you failed to do.

Parents should try to do as much research on ADHD as possible and find out all they can about it. Information also helps to make you less fearful as you will no longer be dealing with the unknown. Find out about any new studies and findings, read articles in medical journals and magazines, and attend lectures on the subject. Find out about the latest treatments that are available to your child. Keep updating your information so you always know when new discoveries are made. Make use of organizations such as the Attention Deficit Disorder Association or the National Institute of Mental Health.

Support

Join ADHD organizations such as Children and Adults with Attention Deficit/Hyperactivity Disorder (CHADD) so you can share your stories with other parents and learn from theirs. No one can teach you as much about raising a child with ADHD as someone who is doing or has done it. When you have a child with special needs especially one like ADHD which can affect your child's ability to socialize, you can end up feeling quite alone, like no one else is experiencing what you are going through. When you join a support group, that feeling goes away because everyone you meet will be dealing with the same or similar challenges that you are. You can usually get referrals from the child's doctors for support groups or places that you can receive counseling on how to deal with the disorder.

It is important to listen to the medical professionals regarding your child's disorder because they are the experts. However, don't be afraid to ask questions to the doctors and therapists in your child's life. Whenever possible get written reports and evaluations, so you can build up a file on your child's development that you can refer to later on or present to educators and anyone else who may need a history. Also keep records of any tests take or medication diagnosed.

Try to get help from the best people. While this may be constrained by a lack of finances, make full use of health insurance and any other assistance that may be available to ensure that your child deals with the best. Your doctor should have some training in pediatrics along with his specialty. It is not advisable to try unproven medication such as herbal remedies or other treatment for your child. Check with the medical professionals before embarking on any new treatment. Many people will come to you with treatments that they insist are revolutionary. Be very careful; do not experiment with your child's health.

Although listening to the professionals is very important it is also crucial that they listen to you. Your child is an individual with his own unique personality and behavior not a case study. Let them know when they are going wrong. Studies have shown that the parents of children with

ADHD are much more in tune with their children than other people, so in a way you are also an expert. Ensure that the medical personnel know what's happening in the home away from their offices by giving them regular updates. Keep track of everything your child does in terms of development and behavioral changes.

If there are two parents involved try your best to work as a team. It is important to support each other and for both of you to support your child. You have to present a unified front. You should appear to be moving forward together and not be going off in different directions. Having a child with ADHD can put strain on a marriage, so parents might want to consider joining a support group or attending therapy sessions, if things start to get problematic. Accept that having someone to talk to is very important. Try to make time on a regular basis for the two of you to get away if only to grab dinner or a movie. Remember that in order to be there for your child, you have to be able to sort through your own issues. Many caregivers and parents forget about their own needs and those of their spouses in their desire to ensure that their child gets all the attention and support that he needs. This might work for a while then you will fall ill and not be able to help anyone. Ensure that you are healthy yourself. Maintain a healthy diet, eat regularly and try to get in some exercise. Make sure that you get enough rest at night so that you can face the next day, which is almost certain to bring more challenges.

When there is a child with ADHD in the home, everyone has to get involved and be on board with his care and treatment. Even aunts and uncles and grandparents have a part to play and do, as well as the other children who live in the home.

When you feel like you can't cope, don't be too proud to ask for help. Don't be ashamed to enlist professional help on those days when the challenges of parenting a child with ADHD become too much. Apart from helping you to cope, a professional can help you work with your child to help him to achieve his full potential.

If there is only one parent, you will have to enlist the help of relatives and friends you can trust when you need a break, which you will need sometimes. Take time for yourself when you can, and don't feel bad about doing it. Single parents are sometimes tempted to give up everything in their lives to dedicate themselves to looking after their child who has ADHD. This is a recipe for problems as you also have needs that must be met. Make time to date or go out with friends, spend time with adults, meet people and have fun. If you are happier your child will be too. Make sure that you take a break before you reach your breaking point because by then it might be too late. Also arrange to spend time with your other children, if you have, and make it one on one if possible. As much as you love your child with ADHD, dealing with him on a daily basis can be draining. Just like any other caregiver, if you do not make sure that you are healthy in mind and body, you cannot fully be there for the other person. So take the time to recharge your batteries.

If you are feeling and perhaps unknowingly expressing negative emotions such as anger or depression, your child can sometimes pick up on that and respond in by acting out. Keep a check on yourself and how you feel. Be in touch with your emotions rather than trying to suppress them because if you don't, you might be contributing to your child's bad behavior without even realizing it.

Once you learn that your child has ADHD, you need to begin training to deal with it. Luckily there are courses that parents can take that prepare them for dealing with the challenges that they are about to face. It is a good idea to sign up for what is called Parental Training which teaches parents ways to deal with having a child with ADHD and strategies for helping them to be the best they can be. Attending therapy right at the very beginning of your journey with your child's ADHD will teach you to anticipate the issues that can arise and allow you to prepare to deal with them. You will be taught how to respond when your child's behavior becomes disruptive which is almost sure to happen from time to time.

Stay Positive

There will be days that are more challenging than others; try always to look on the positive side and don't despair. Try to always remember that your child is seldom upsetting you deliberately. They often cannot change their behavior on their own even if they may want to. This will be frustrating for them as well as for you. Remain hopeful but be realistic as well about what can and cannot be achieved. Monitoring and meeting the needs of the child with ADHD can be physically and psychologically exhausting, as well as a source of frustration, because the results you want could take a long time or never happen at all. You can find yourself feeling worried or fearful all the time especially if the child is away from the home without you. You worry that he might be injured because children with ADHD can sometimes be quite restless. You fear that someone might take advantage of him and want to be there for him all the time, but this is not possible. It is not what is best for the child and trying to achieve it can wear you out.

One of the mistakes parents make is trying to fix everything at once. There are many behaviors and situations arising out of your child's disorder. Tackle them one by one. That is going to require a great deal of patience but it is the only way to move forward without becoming frustrated.

Try to enjoy the time you spend with your child, and do not spend all your time together worrying about what could happen or what is to come. If you do that, you could lose sight of the wonderful person that is your child, and all the things you can learn from him. Also, try not to demand too much of yourself, accept that

you will make mistakes that you will not
be fully in control of every situation.

Chapter 8: An Overview

ADHD is neither a "new" mental health problem nor is it a disorder created for the purpose of personal gain or financial profit by pharmaceutical companies, the mental health field, or by the media. It is a very real behavioral and medical disorder that affects millions of people nationwide. According to the National Institute of Mental Health (NIMH), ADHD is one of the most common mental disorders in children and adolescents. According to NIMH, the estimated number of children with ADHD is between 3% - 5% of the population. NIMH also estimates 4.1 percent of adults have ADHD.

Although it has taken quite some time for our society to accept ADHD as a bonafide mental health and/or medical disorder, in actuality it is a problem that has been noted in modern literature for at least 200 years. As early as 1798, ADHD was first described in the medical literature by Dr. Alexander Crichton, who referred to it as

"Mental Restlessness." A tale of an apparent ADHD youth, "The Story of Fidgety Philip," was written in 1845 by Dr. Heinrich Hoffman. In 1922, ADHD was recognized as Post Encephalitic Behavior Disorder. In 1937, it was discovered that stimulants helped control hyperactivity in children. In 1957, methylphenidate (Ritalin), became commercially available to treat hyperactive children.

The formal and accepted mental health/behavioral diagnosis of ADHD is relatively recent. In the early 1960s, ADHD was referred to as "Minimal Brain Dysfunction." In 1968, the disorder became known as "Hyperkinetic Reaction of Childhood." At this point, emphasis was placed more on the hyperactivity than inattention symptoms.

In 1980, the diagnosis was changed to "ADD--Attention Deficit Disorder, with or without Hyperactivity," which placed equal emphasis on hyperactivity and inattention. By 1987, the disorder was renamed Attention Deficit Hyperactivity Disorder

(ADHD) and was subdivided into four categories (see below). Since then, ADHD has been considered a medical disorder that results in behavioral problems.

Currently, ADHD is defined by the DSM IV-TR (the accepted diagnostic manual) as one disorder subdivided into four categories:

1.   Attention-Deficit/Hyperactivity Disorder, Predominantly Inattentive Type (previously known as ADD) is marked by impaired attention and concentration.

2.   Attention-Deficit/Hyperactivity Disorder, Predominantly Hyperactive, Impulsive Type (formerly known as ADHD) is marked by hyperactivity without inattentiveness.

3.   Attention-Deficit/Hyperactivity Disorder, Combined Type (the most common type) involves all the symptoms: inattention, hyperactivity, and impulsivity.

4. Attention-Deficit/Hyperactivity Disorder Not Otherwise Specified. This category is for the ADHD disorders that include

prominent symptoms of inattention or hyperactivity-impulsivity, but do not meet the DSM IV-TR criteria for a diagnosis.

To further understand ADHD and its four subcategories, it helps to illustrate hyperactivity, impulsivity, and/or inattention through examples.

Typical hyperactive symptoms in youth include:

Often "on the go" or acting as if "driven by a motor"

Feeling restless

Moving hands and feet nervously or squirming

Getting up frequently to walk or run around

Running or climbing excessively when it's inappropriate

Having difficulty playing quietly or engaging in quiet leisure activities

Talking excessively or too fast

Often leaving their seat when staying seated is expected

Often can't be involved in social activities quietly

Typical symptoms of impulsivity in youth include:

Acting rashly or suddenly without thinking first

Blurting out answers before questions are fully asked

Having a difficult time awaiting their turn

Often interrupting others' conversations or activities

Poor judgment or decisions in social situations, which result in the child not being accepted by his/her own peer group.

Typical symptoms of inattention in youth include:

Not paying attention to details or makes careless mistakes

Having trouble staying focused and being easily distracted

Appearing not to listen when spoken to

Often forgetful in daily activities

Having trouble staying organized, planning ahead, and finishing projects

Losing or misplacing homework, books, toys, or other items

Not seeming to listen when directly spoken to

Not following instructions and failing to finish activities, schoolwork, chores or duties in the workplace

Avoiding or disliking tasks that require ongoing mental effort or concentration

Of the four ADHD subcategories, Hyperactive-Impulsive Type is the most distinguishable, recognizable, and the easiest to diagnose. The hyperactive and impulsive symptoms are behaviorally manifested in the various environments in which a child interacts: i.e., at home, with friends, at school, and/or during extracurricular or athletic activities.

Because of the hyperactive and impulsive traits of this subcategory, these children naturally arouse the attention (often negative) of those around them.

Compared to children without ADHD, they are more difficult to instruct, teach, coach, and to communicate with. Additionally, they are prone to be disruptive, seemingly oppositional, reckless, accident prone, and are socially underdeveloped.

Parents of ADHD youth often report frustration, anger, and emotional depletion because of their child's inattention, impulsivity, and hyperactivity. By the time they receive professional services many parents of ADHD children describe complex feelings of anger, fear, desperation, and guilt. Their multiple "failures" at getting their children to focus, pay attention, and to follow through with directions, responsibilities, and assignments have resulted in feelings of hopelessness and desperation.

These parents often report feeling guilty over their resentment, loss of patience, and reactive discipline style. Both psychotherapists and psychiatrists have worked with parents of ADHD youth who "joke" by saying "if someone doesn't help my child, give me some medication!"

The following statistics (Dr. Russel Barkley and Dr. Tim Willens) illustrate the far reaching implications of ADHD in youth.

ADHD has a childhood rate of occurrence of 6-8%, with the illness continuing into adolescence for 75% of the patients, and with 50% of cases persisting into adulthood.

Boys are diagnosed with ADHD 3 times more often than girls.

Emotional development in children with ADHD is 30% slower than in their non-ADHD peers.

65% of children with ADHD exhibit problems in defiance or problems with authority figures. This can include verbal hostility and temper tantrums.

Teenagers with ADHD have almost four times as many traffic citations as non-ADD/ADHD drivers. They have four times as many car accidents and are seven times more likely to have a second accident.

21% of teens with ADHD skip school on a regular basis, and 35% drop out of school before finishing high school.

45% of children with ADHD have been suspended from school at least once.

30% of children with ADHD have repeated a year of school.

Youth treated with medication have a six-fold less chance of developing a substance abuse disorder through adolescence.

The juvenile justice system is composed of 75% of kids with undiagnosed learning disabilities, including ADHD.

ADHD is a genetically transmitted disorder. Research funded by the National Institute of Medical Health (NIMH) and the U.S. Public Health Service (PHS) have shown clear evidence that ADHD runs in families. According to recent research, over 25% of first-degree relatives of the families of ADHD children also have ADHD. Other research indicates that 80% of adults with ADHD have at least one child with ADHD and 52% have two or more children with ADHD.

The hereditary link to ADHD has important treatment implications because other children in a family may also have ADHD. Moreover, there is a distinct possibility the parents also may have ADHD. Of course, matters get complicated when parents with undiagnosed ADHD have problems with their ADHD child. Therefore, it is crucial to evaluate a family occurrence of ADHD, when assessing ADHD in youth.

Diagnosing Attention Deficit Disorder Inattentive Type in youth is no easy task. More harm than good is done when a person is incorrectly diagnosed. A wrong diagnosis may lead to unnecessary treatment, i.e., a prescription for ADHD medication and/or unnecessary psychological, behavioral and/or educational services. Unnecessary treatment like ADHD medication may be emotionally and physically harmful. Conversely, when an individual is correctly diagnosed and subsequently treated for

ADHD, the potential for dramatic life changes are limitless.

A medical doctor (preferably a psychiatrist) or another licensed, trained, and qualified mental health professional can diagnose ADHD. Only certain medical professionals can prescribe medication. These are physicians (M.D. or D.O.), nurse practitioners, and physician assistants (P.A.) under the supervision of a physician. However, psychiatrists, because of their training and expertise in mental health disorders, are the best qualified to prescribe ADHD medication.

While the ADHD Hyperactive Type youth are easily noticed, those with ADHD Inattentive Type are prone to be misdiagnosed or, worse, do not even get noticed. Moreover, ADHD Inattentive Type youth are often mislabeled, misunderstood, and even blamed for a disorder over which they have no control. Because ADHD Inattentive Type manifests more internally and less behaviorally, these youth are not as frequently flagged by potential treatment providers.

Therefore, these youth often do not receive potentially life-enhancing treatment, i.e., psychotherapy, school counseling/coaching, educational services, and/or medical/psychiatric services. Unfortunately, many "fall between the cracks" of the social service, mental health, juvenile justice, and educational systems.

Youth with unrecognized and untreated ADHD may develop into adults with poor self-concepts low self-esteem, associated emotional, educational, and employment problems. According to reliable statistics, adults with unrecognized and/or untreated ADHD are more prone to develop alcohol and drug problems. It is common for adolescents and adults with ADHD to attempt to soothe or "self medicate" themselves by using addictive substances such as alcohol, marijuana, narcotics, tranquilizers, nicotine, cocaine and illegally prescribed drugs or street amphetamines (stimulants).

Approximately 60% of people who had ADHD symptoms as a child continue to have symptoms as adults. And only 1 in 4 of adults with ADHD were diagnosed in childhood-and even fewer are treated. Thanks to increased public awareness and the pharmaceutical corporations' marketing of their medications, more adults are now seeking help for ADHD.

However, many of these adults who were not treated as children carry emotional, educational, personal, and occupational "scars." As children, these individuals, did not feel "as smart, successful and/or likable" as their non ADHD counterparts. With no one to explain why they struggled at home, with friends, and in school, they naturally turned inward to explain their deficiencies. Eventually they internalize the negative messages about themselves, thereby creating fewer opportunities for success as adults.

Similarly to youths, adults with ADHD have serious problems with concentration or paying attention, or are overactive (hyperactive) in one or more areas of living. Some of the most common problems include:

Problems with jobs or careers; losing or quitting jobs frequently

Problems doing as well as you should at work or in school

Problems with day-to-day tasks such as doing household chores, paying bills, and organizing things

Problems with relationships because you forget important things, can't finish tasks, or get upset over little things

Ongoing stress and worry because you don't meet goals and responsibilities

Ongoing, strong feelings of frustration, guilt, or blame

According to Adult ADHD research:

ADHD may affect 30% of people who had ADHD in childhood.

ADHD does not develop in adulthood. Only those who have had the disorder since early childhood really suffer from ADHD.

A key criterion of ADHD in adults is "disinhibition"--the inability to stop acting on impulse. Hyperactivity is much less likely to be a symptom of the disorder in adulthood.

Adults with ADHD tend to forget appointments and are frequently socially inappropriate--making rude or insulting remarks--and are disorganized. They find prioritizing difficult.

Adults with ADHD find it difficult to form lasting relationships.

Adults with ADHD have problems with short-term memory. Almost all people with ADHD suffer other psychological problems--particularly depression and substance abuse.

While there is not a consensus as to the cause of ADHD, there is a general agreement within the medical and mental health communities that it is biological in nature. Some common explanations for ADHD include: chemical imbalance in the brain, nutritional deficiencies, early head trauma/brain injury, or impediments to normal brain development (i.e. the use of cigarettes and alcohol during pregnancy).

ADHD may also be caused by brain dysfunction or neurological impairment. Dysfunction in the areas in the frontal lobes, basal ganglia, and cerebellum may negatively impact regulation of behavior, inhibition, short-term memory, planning, self-monitoring, verbal regulation, motor control, and emotional regulation.

Because successful treatment of this disorder can have profound positive emotional, social, and family outcomes, an accurate diagnosis is tremendously important. Requirements to diagnose ADHD include: professional education (graduate and post graduate), ongoing training, supervision, experience, and licensure. Even with the essential professional qualifications, collaboration and input from current or former psychotherapists, parents, teachers, school staff, medical practitioners and/or psychiatrists create more reliable and accurate diagnoses. The value of collaboration cannot be understated.

Sound ethical practice compels clinicians to provide the least restrictive and least risky form of therapy/treatment to youth with ADHD. Medication or intensive psycho-therapeutic services should only be provided when the client would not favorably respond to less invasive treatment approaches. Therefore, it is crucial to determine whether "functional impairment" is or is not present.

Clients who are functionally impaired will fail to be successful in their environment without specialized assistance, services, and/or psycho-therapeutic or medical treatment. Once functional impairment is established, then it is the job of the treatment team to collaborate on the most effective method of treatment.

All too often, a person is mistakenly diagnosed with ADHD, not due to attention deficit issues, but rather because of their unique personality, learning style, emotional make-up, energy and activity levels, and other psycho-social factors that better explain their problematic behaviors. A misdiagnosis could also be related to other mental or emotional conditions (discussed next), a life circumstance including a parent's unemployment, divorce, family dysfunction, or medical conditions. In a small but significant number of cases, this diagnosis of ADHD better represents an adult's need to manage a challenging, willful and oppositional child, who even with these problems may not have ADHD.

It is critical that before an ADHD diagnosis is reached (especially before medication is prescribed), that a clinician consider if other coexisting mental or medical disorders may be responsible for the hyperactive, impulsive, and/or inattentive symptoms. Because other disorders share similar symptoms with ADHD, it is necessary to consider the probability of one mental/psychological disorder over that of another that could possibly account for a client's symptoms.

For example, Generalized Anxiety Disorder and Major Depression share the symptoms of disorganization, lack of concentration, and work completion issues. A trained and qualified ADHD specialist will consider differential diagnoses in order to arrive at the most logical and clinically sound diagnosis. Typical disorders to be ruled out include: Generalized Anxiety, Major Depression, Post Traumatic Stress Disorder, and Substance Abuse Disorders. Additionally, medical explanations should be similarly sought: sleep disorders, nutritional deficiencies, hearing impairment, and others.

When a non-medical practitioner formally diagnoses a client with ADHD, i.e. a licensed psychotherapist, it is recommended that a second opinion (or confirmation of the diagnosis) be sought from a psychiatrist. Psychiatrists are medical practitioners who specialize in the medical side of mental disorders. Psychiatrists can prescribe medicine that may be necessary to treat ADHD. In collaboration, the parents, school personnel, the referring psychotherapist, and the psychiatrist, will monitor the effectiveness of the medical component of the ADHD treatment.

Chapter 9: Ensure Proper Nutrition For Your Child

Although your child's condition is not a direct result of his diet, what he eats has an impact on his mental state as well as his behavior. It will be in your child's favor if you make sure to monitor and make the necessary changes to the kinds of food he eats, the times he eats, and the amount of food he consumes. The payoff will be your child's reduced ADHD symptoms.

Nix Unhealthy Eating Habits

Kids with ADHD tend to miss their meals. As a result of not eating regularly, they later overeat whatever they could lay their hands on. This unhealthy eating pattern has a negative impact on their physical as well as emotional health.

Your child's physical health will benefit from consuming fresh foods, following scheduled meal times, and avoiding all forms of junk food. Regular meal times will also benefit his mental health, as they serve as necessary breaks as well as provide rhythm to his day.

To avoid developing unhealthy eating habits:

1. See to it that your child has regular balanced meals and snacks, which should be scheduled no more than 3 hours apart.

2. Eliminate all forms of junk food in your pantry and refrigerator.

3. Have your child take a vitamin and mineral supplement each day.

4. It would also be helpful to steer clear of the TV when you know there will be usual onslaught of junk food commercials.

5. When going out to eat, make sure to ignore the fatty and sugary offerings.

Hooray for Healthy Eating Habits

Your child will naturally be drawn to foods that he enjoys eating the most. Help him develop healthy eating habits by taking steps to entice him with nutritious options.

1. Prepare more homemade meals.

Meals that you eat in restaurants or buy on takeout contain more unhealthy fats and added sugars. It will do your child's healthy plenty of good to cook your meals at home instead. Preparing homemade meals in big batches also lets you cut down on the number of times you have to cook. You can then focus on your child's other needs when you know that you have made enough to feed your family for an entire week.

2. Curb portion sizes.

Doing this will help stop you from insisting that your child eat everything on his plate. Remember also to avoid rewarding or bribing your child with food.

3. Hide healthier foods in tasty dishes.

Stir veggies into your child's favorite beef stew.

Smother apple slices in a delicious dip.

Mash those carrots together with his much-loved potatoes.

Blend shredded vegetables into sauces.

Prepare zucchini muffins, carrot bread, and cheesy cauliflower casserole.

4. Let your child help you shop for groceries and prepare the meals.

This way, you get to teach him about various kinds of foods and how to read labels on food packages. The best thing about this is that you get to spend quality time together. Letting him select the produce also encourages him to help you cook the meal. And because he had something to do with preparing the dish, he would also be more eager to eat it.

5. Pay attention to your child's overall diet.

Avoid focusing on specific foods. Although you do have to keep in mind that your child has to consume more whole foods and less processed ones.

6. Practice what you preach about food choices.

You will have more success in encouraging your child to eat his healthy veggies if he sees you passing up those potato chips and munching on carrot sticks instead.

Always Start Your Child's Day with Breakfast

Eating breakfast regularly lets your child have higher energy and more stabilized moods. You can also help him maintain his ideal weight if you make sure to provide him a protein-rich breakfast.

1. Choose high quality proteins. Think milk, yogurt, cheese, fish, eggs, meat, and enriched cereals.

2. Boil some eggs on Sunday. Then, during those weekdays when you are pressed for time, give them to your child to eat along with an apple and a bowl of high protein cereal (choose the low sugar variant).

3. Add variety to your child's breakfast.

Give him a breakfast burrito filled with chicken/beef, cheese, and scrambled eggs. You may also freeze several breakfast burritos to reheat later in the week.

Spread his favorite peanut butter on toast (choose whole grain).

Prepare a simple yet tasty egg sandwich and serve it with a pot of cottage cheese or Greek yogurt.

Tempt Your Child with New Foods

If your child is a picky eater, know that you can "advertise" new tastes to his palate without breaking a sweat. Just follow these tips:

1. When introducing your child to new food items, do so one at a time.

2. Control his intake of snacks and beverages so that he is not filled up before the next meal.

3. Stash plenty of fresh veggie and fruit snacks at home. Make it easier for your child to eat them willingly by ensuring they are washed and cut up into unusual shapes – think yellow squash in the shape of a sun, cauliflower pieces that are formed like clouds, and broccoli florets that look like trees. Then let him eat them with hummus, nut butter, or yogurt for added protein.

4. The easiest way to include vegetables in your child's list of favorite foods is to serve it along with what he already loves. Go ahead and add lentils to his most wanted chowder.

5. After limiting his snacks the whole day, he will be hungry by evening – that would be the best time to give him the new food.

Dodge the "Moody" Foods

Some foods can cause your child to have bad moods. Make sure to avoid giving him:

Highly processed foods – these include any food item made from refined flour, sweet desserts and other sugary treats, and fried foods.

Caffeine-containing beverages such as soft drinks, coffee drinks, and energy drinks.

Sweetened fruit drinks

Diet sodas

Curb the Simple Carbs

Refined grains and sugars are referred to as simple carbohydrates because all nutrients, bran, and fiber have been removed from them. Simple carbs include pasta, white flour, white bread, a large number of breakfast cereals, white rice, pastries, and pizza dough, and all of these can cause your child's blood sugar level to spike to such dangerous levels that his mood and energy fluctuate accordingly.

Your child already gets the sugar his body needs from those that naturally occur in the foods he eats. Letting him consume added sugar simply means he is eating empty calories that do not only increase his risk for type 2 diabetes and obesity, but also contribute to his mood swings and hyperactivity.

It would be best to give your child complex carbs. With their high fiber and nutrient content, they are digested slowly by the body and give your child more energy that lasts for longer. Make sure to include non-starchy veggies, brown rice, beans, high-fiber cereals, whole wheat bread, multigrain bread, fruit, and nuts.

It would also be helpful to limit your child's sugar intake:

1. Say no to sugary drinks.

Entice your child instead with sparkling water splashed with a little fruit juice. You could also make him a yummy mixed berry smoothie or a milkshake made with bananas and whole milk.

2. Tweak your beloved recipes.

With a little makeover, your recipes will surely taste just as delicious with only a little sugar in them.

3. Prepare homemade popsicles.

Let your child enjoy his frozen treats without worrying about his sugar intake by filling ice cube trays with fruit juice (100%), adding the popsicle handles (or plastic spoons), and then freezing.

4. Try making frozen fruit kebabs.

Your kid will surely enjoy noshing on them, especially if you make them using grapes, pineapple chunks, berries, and bananas.

5. Avoid putting up the No Sweets rule.

Banning sweets entirely only makes them more tempting to your child, making it more likely for him to binge on them when he gets the chance.

Practice Smart Fat Consumption

Your child actually needs lots of healthy fats in his diet, as they help him improve his mood and stay full. Just remember to:

1. Go for the healthy fats.

Healthy fats refer to:

Monounsaturated fats that include avocados, seeds (like sesame seeds and pumpkin seeds), nuts (such as almonds, pecans, and hazelnuts), and olive oil.

Polyunsaturated fats that include the omega-3s, which are found in salmon, mackerel, sardines, herring, anchovies, and other fatty fish, as well as in walnuts and flaxseed.

2. Unhealthy fats

These are the trans fats, of which no amount is considered safe. They are found in:

Some margarines

Vegetable shortenings

Processed foods (trans fat free or otherwise), including snack foods, candies, baked goods like crackers and cookies, and fried foods.

Go for Healthy Snacks

Your child may find snacking on junk food to be too tempting to pass up. Fortunately, there is an effective way of going around the sugary, unhealthy-fat-loaded, calorie-laden, and nutrient-deficient route, and that is by giving your kid healthier snack alternatives.

Let your child try the following healthy snack substitutions:

Oven-baked and lightly salted potato fries instead of French fries

Fresh fruit smoothies, homemade sorbets, and Greek yogurt instead of ice cream

Grilled chicken instead of fried chicken

Low-sugar homemade cakes and cookies, English muffins, and bagels instead of doughnuts

Vanilla wafers, graham crackers, fruity caramel dip, and fig bars instead of chocolate chip cookies

Nuts and baked veggie chips instead of potato chips

Sit Down for Meals with Your Child

Apart from making sure that your child eats healthy food, sitting down with your child and other family members provides the following benefits:

It provides comfort to your child. He will feel comforted by the fact that the entire family regularly comes together to enjoy the food and simply bask in each other's company. This actually enhances your child's appetite and encourages him to eat better.

It gives you a chance to get updated about your kid's life at home and in school. The dinner table is one of those places where you can truly communicate with your child

— talking with and listening to him without being distracted by phones, computers, or the television.

It provides an opportunity for your child to have social interaction. Simply talking to you and to other family members while sitting down to a healthy meal, especially when he gets to talk about how he feels about certain things, has a big impact on your child's self-esteem, stress level, and mood. Having social interactions with your kid at the dinner table also allows you to have a good grasp on your child's issues so that you could better help him cope with them.

It lets you teach your kid about healthy eating — without bring preachy about it. When you regularly eat together with your child and the rest of the family, he has no choice but to always watch you consume healthy food in controlled portions. Keep in mind that it helps not to talk about your own weight issues or to obsess about the number of calories in whatever you are eating at the dinner table. Doing this will ensure that your child does not inadvertently develop negative ideas about food.

It allows you to check on how your child actually eats. This is particularly important for when your child is at that age when he eats a lot at school. Make sure to instill in your kid the results of frequently eating unhealthy food choices in excessive amounts as well as the nutritional and physical advantages of having a balanced diet.

Chapter 10: Symptoms And Myths Of Adult Adhd

One of the most important elements of coping with adult ADHD successfully is understanding the condition and how it can impact your daily life. Too often people with ADHD give into negative thinking about their difficulties with performing seemingly simple tasks and managing the demands of daily life, thinking that they are simply lazy or not trying hard enough. However, many of the symptoms of ADHD are the culprits behind this behavior. When people realize they have a condition that makes it hard for them to prioritize, organize, and stay focused, they can release the negativity and work with their condition, rather than struggle against it.

Even for those who suspect that they have adult ADHD, recognizing the symptoms can be difficult. There are a lot of myths surrounding adult ADHD that serve to confuse people about its legitimacy and seriousness. Moreover, this misinformation increases the stigma in our society around the acceptance of mental health disorders, which further alienates those who already struggle with meeting society's standards. These myths greatly discourage people from seeking help, getting a diagnosis, and receiving the treatment that they need.

On the other hand, the confusion surrounding adult ADHD can lead some to mistake their behavior for that of adult ADHD symptoms. Plenty of people have a hard time focusing on tasks that they find tedious or uninteresting, and lots of others struggle with getting organized and executing good time management—these are the basic struggles of the human condition, it seems. However, those with adult ADHD have a marked difference in their behavior, which is majorly disruptive and biologically caused. To remedy this confusion, let's take a look at some of the facts and myths about adult ADHD.

What is adult ADHD?

Attention Deficit Hyperactive Disorder (ADHD) is a neurochemical imbalance that makes it difficult for the sufferer to focus on tasks, to prioritize and organize their lives, and to maintain a calm, focused disposition. ADHD usually begins in early childhood, and symptoms often dissipate with age. However, many experience symptoms continuing into adolescence and adulthood, with 70% of those who exhibited ADHD symptoms continuing to experience them into adolescence, and 50% having them continue into adulthood.

Many people who don't receive a diagnosis until they are adults may have had ADHD for most of their lives without realizing it. Doctors don't know what exactly causes ADHD, but it is believed that genetic disposition, environmental exposure to substances like lead in early development, and exposure to toxic substances like drugs and cigarettes in utero may be factors.

ADHD is caused by an imbalance in the brain that blocks the reception of dopamine by neurotransmitters. When this occurs, the reward system of the brain is inhibited, so that those who have this imbalance are not getting the neurochemical payoff that those without it do. Those with ADHD then seek harder for experiences that give them that dopamine spike to make up for the imbalance. Dopamine is released during novel experiences, leading ADHD sufferers to seek constant stimulation and change. This inability to receive chemical rewards the way others do also makes it difficult to focus on tasks that do not provide an immediate payoff.

Psychiatrists often prescribe drugs like psychostimulants to help redirect the brain's chemicals to where they need to go. While many find success with prescription treatment, others dispute whether this is the best way to go. It is important to talk with your doctor before deciding to start or discontinue prescriptions of any kind.

Symptoms

While everyone experiences the symptoms of adult ADHD differently, the signs are generally the same. There is a marked difference between how the symptoms appear in males as opposed to females. Men are more likely to be hyperactive as children, unable to slow down and focus. Symptoms tend to subside with age.

Women, on the other hand, may not start showing symptoms until the onset of puberty, when the increase of estrogen changes the brain's chemistry. While men tend to experience ADHD more as a sense of restlessness and distraction, it tends to manifest more in women as severe disorganization and forgetfulness.

People of both genders, however, experience all symptoms to some degree. Here are the general symptoms of adult ADHD:

Extreme difficulty with getting and staying organized due to the inability to focus on tasks. This leads to missed appointments, unpaid bills, missed deadlines, and losing important items frequently, like keys, credit cards, cellphones, wallets, important documents, etc.

Issues with prioritizing tasks.

Poor planning skills.

Trouble starting tasks.

Being easily distracted, which makes it hard to focus on and complete important tasks.

Impulsiveness. This can be dangerous in many cases when people with ADHD participate in reckless behavior like abusing substances, getting in trouble with the law, engaging in promiscuous sex, and reckless driving.

Frequently being late.

Poor listening skills.

Struggles with relationships due to trouble with listening and honoring commitments.

Sudden mood swings and outbursts.

Becoming easily frustrated and hot tempered.

Trouble coping with stress.

Restlessness and trouble sleeping or relaxing.

Learning disabilities.

Low self-esteem.

ADHD is often accompanied by other mood disorders, such as anxiety or depression.

Myths

No one really knows how myths get started, but when it comes to mental illness, myths only cause harm for those who suffer from mental illness and the people who love, live, and work with them. Fortunately, debunking the myths can help clear up any confusion and leads to greater understanding for those seeking to cope with their symptoms and the people who want to support them.

The following are common myths surrounding adult ADHD, and their corrected answers.

ADHD is not a real medical disorder.

Yes, it is. ADHD causes neurobiological symptoms that result from a chemical imbalance in the brain.

ADHD is just an excuse.

ADHD is a disability that makes it difficult for those who have it to perform to the levels of those who do not. People with ADHD often need special accommodations to help them learn and work more efficiently. These accommodations are necessary for helping them to level the playing field so that they can succeed, rather than try to meet expectations when starting out at a severe disadvantage. Again, ADHD is a real medical disorder with symptoms that come naturally as a result of the neurochemical imbalance in the brain.

Children with ADHD will always outgrow it.

False. As we saw earlier, 70% of children who have ADHD will continue to experience symptoms into adolescence, and 50% will experience them into adulthood. The majority of adults with ADHD go undiagnosed if symptoms were not recognized during childhood, and many of them also struggle with other mood disorders like anxiety and depression.

ADHD only affects boys.

ADHD affects both males and females, though as we saw earlier, the symptoms often manifest differently.

Medication for ADHD turns patients into zombies.

When prescribed at the appropriate dosages, prescription medications for ADHD work to correct the imbalance of chemicals in the brain. These prescriptions will help boost the receptivity of neurotransmitters and block the transport of dopamine back into the brain's neurons, helping to increase dopamine levels in the brain. This, in turn, helps the patient to stay calm and focused.

It can take a while for a patient and doctor to find the dosage level that works just right. The adjustment period for any medication that affects the brain's neurochemistry will often cause various symptoms, but these should generally only be temporary.

In addition, patients who were previously hyperactive, restless, and impulsive will no longer feel the chemical need to receive stimulation and engage in their prior behavior when the chemical imbalance is corrected. This could create a marked difference in the patient's personality to others, but these "character traits" are actually medical symptoms that are being treated.

ADHD is the result of bad parenting/lack of childhood discipline.

Again, ADHD is a medical condition. Some parenting techniques may certainly exacerbate the child's symptoms, but for other patients, no amount of discipline and hard expectations can help them to overcome their symptoms unless accommodations are made to work around the condition.

Sometimes the symptoms of ADHD are masked by strong organization and structure provided by the parents. It is when the structure of early family life falls away that individuals suddenly struggle to recreate that same organization for themselves. This can explain why many are not diagnosed with ADHD until reaching adulthood. Even the best parenting in the world cannot correct the symptoms of ADHD if parents did not educate their children about their conditions and teach them strong coping skills.

People with ADHD are stupid, lazy, or simply disobedient.

Many people with ADHD are actually of above-average intelligence, and they can be high achievers when they understand how to properly accommodate their needs. Their seeming lack of motivation is simply an inability to stay focused when short-term rewards are not available. Without this instantaneous payoff, people with ADHD can have a hard time achieving long-term goals and planning for the future.

However, when engaging in activities that provide high amounts of pleasure and/or constant stimulation, individuals with ADHD can maintain a laser-like focus on the activity for hours. People simply need to know how to work with their reward systems to help stay focused and motivated.

There are certainly many more myths surrounding ADHD, and the nuances of symptoms are complex and unique to the individual. A long talk with one's doctor or psychiatrist can help clear up further questions and dig deeper to determine the many symptoms of ADHD.

Chapter 11: Attention Deficit Hyperactivity Disorder How Does It Differ From Add

Attention Deficit Hyperactivity Disorder usually develops during childhood but it could continue until adolescence and even until adulthood. That is why there are also adults who suffer from **ADHD**. In some cases, adults have not realized they have **ADHD** during their childhood years and were only able to learn that they have the disorder when they have reached such an age.

Children who have ADHD show signs of inattention, overactivity or hyperactivity, and impulsive behaviour. Thus, this disorder is classified into three types: ADHD inattentive, ADHD hyperactive-impulsive, and a combination of the three, which is the most common type. ADHD inattentive children often show difficulty in sustaining focus and attention, are sluggish and are often drowsy, and often seem to be lost in a daydream.

Meanwhile, ADHD hyperactive-impulsive children are often over-active and always on the move, seem to talk endlessly and have difficulty controlling their emotions and may often have temperamental outbursts.

Attention Deficit Hyperactivity Disorder is sometimes confused with and used interchangeably with Attention Deficit Disorder (ADD). However, these two terms are in a way different. Attention Deficit Disorder is the general term used to refer to the behavioural disorder of childhood that shows symptoms of ADHD but do not have the impulsive and hyperactive behaviours. ADHD is a subtype of ADD.

The Three Types of ADD or ADHD

ADD or ADHD is classified into three separate categories. These are the hyperactive-impulsive type, the inattentive type, and the combined type and are as follows:

Hyperactive-Impulsive Type - In the case where the ADD or ADHD is predominantly the hyperactive and impulsive type, the symptoms are related primarily to hyperactivity and impulsivity and do not typically any significant attention issues. These individuals are fidgety and impulsive while also being overactive and restless.

They will usually blurt things out, usually interrupting others by acting and speaking before they think. They have considerable difficulty staying seated, talking excessively, and waiting for their turns.

Inattentive Type - with this type of ADD or ADHD, the symptoms are primarily related to the inability of the person to pay attention. The inattentive form of the disorder is usually referred to as ADD rather than ADHD. The individuals with this form of the disorder have difficulty finishing tasks, following directions, and paying attention. They appear to be careless as well as disorganized and forgetful, they become distracted easily, and they frequently lose things.

Combined Type - the combined type is the easiest of the three to diagnosis because the characteristics of the two types mentioned above are all present.

The most important point with **ADD or ADHD** is that once the disorder has been properly diagnosed, the correct treatment can be recommended.

Chapter 12: The Abcs Of Adhd

The latest edition of the **Diagnostic and Statistical Manual** (**DSM**) places ADHD sufferers in three basic categories according to the symptoms they exhibit. The **Predominantly Hyperactive-Impulsive** variety of the disorder has received the bulk of the attention from the medical community as it was the first to be widely recognized. It took much longer for experts to realize that there was also a form of the disorder in which sufferers did not display symptoms of hyperactivity. As a result, the **Predominantly Inattentive** type (from which I suffer) has received far less scrutiny. In addition, individuals suffering from the **Combined** type of the disorder exhibit a mixture of both types of symptoms.

Because this book focuses on the Inattentive variety, I believe it is important for readers to recognize some of the most common symptoms of the disorder. Most obvious to others is the tendency of someone with ADHD to daydream, become distracted, or grow bored quickly. These characteristics tie in closely with a difficulty in following instructions properly, trouble grasping important details, and needing longer than usual to process and understand information. Because of the difficulties that these symptoms create for sufferers, they may display a marked inability to keep on task. Difficulty in keeping organized combined with frequent episodes of forgetfulness can make like performing in school and at work difficult. Because these can turn otherwise normal activities into an uphill battle, sufferers often avoid tasks requiring effort. Unfortunately, this sometimes causes others to mistakenly attribute their behaviors to laziness or a lack of motivation.

While many of these traits describe all of us at some point, for people with ADHD, they can often interfere with the ability to live a "normal" and productive life. As with other disorders, only someone who had

ADHD can truly explain how the condition affects them. By sharing my experiences, and providing insight into the difficulties it can create in people's lives, I hope to foster greater understanding between those who struggle daily with the challenges of ADD and those who don't.

Dying for a Diagnosis

Although the symptoms of ADHD had been observed for decades, it wasn't until the 1950s that the term "hyperkinetic impulse disorder" was used to describe the condition responsible for them. In the mid-1960s, "minimal brain dysfunction syndrome" was used to describe kids who had problems with perception, memory, attention and impulse. It was only in 1980 that the **Diagnostic and Statistical Manual** listed "Attention Deficit Disorder" and its various subtypes. With such a short history, our overall understanding of ADHD is nowhere near as broad as that of some other disorders. As a result, misdiagnosis or a lack of diagnosis can pose difficulties which continue to plague sufferers throughout their lives.

When I first began school, ADHD "diagnosis" had gone little beyond academics who studied the symptoms and had as of yet to give the disorder a name. Since the emphasis at that time was on the more obvious displays of hyperactivity, it would be a long while before my behavioral characteristics would be recognized for what they were. While I caused my teachers little trouble (as most of my time was spent staring out of the window) my report cards were peppered with confidence-crippling comments like "does not pay attention," "does not complete homework," and "constantly loses supplies." It's was hardly a promising start to a well-rounded educational experience.

Halfway through my fifth-grade year we moved to another city, where it became apparent that I couldn't keep up in school. I was unable to answer when called on, and when I **remembered** to do my homework, the assignments seemed irrelevant or meaningless. When it was necessary to recall material, it was as if I'd never heard it before. That period stands out in my mind as one marked by frustration and fear.

The school system decided that I was "slow" and placed me in remedial classes, despite the fact that away from class, I was gobbling up Robert Heinlein's science fiction works like lobster on an all-you-can-eat buffet. More advanced and stimulating subject matter was replaced by drudge work, and I'm fairly certain that I've diagrammed more sentences than most people have written in a lifetime. When after just a few weeks in purgatory the whole concept of communication suddenly clicked, I was retested and moved into an honors English class.

That was never that case with math, in which my problems seemed more insurmountable than the high wall on the Marine Corps obstacle course. Concentrating enough to follow instructions was a problem, so I spent a lot of time checking to make sure I was doing things correctly. I was constantly starting equations over because I couldn't remember if I'd entered the right number (or any number at all) or whether I'd completely missed a step somewhere. While I am now able to understand many mathematical concepts well, as soon as specific numbers are thrown into the mix I'm lost. I'm either totally unable to find a solution, or arrive at numerous conflicting ones. As a result, I haven't balanced my checkbook in at least a decade, and I consciously avoid any project that involves applied math. It's an inconvenient and disheartening fact that has shaped my approach to how I do things.

Chapter 13: Treating A Child With Diet

In order to treat a child, of the unpleasant symptoms that ADHD brings to the table, one must identify what foods or additives trigger the response, in order to eliminate them from the diet. The task at hand might seem easy at first, but you are to discover that it's quite challenging. Children tend to have a changing behavior, and what may seem as a symptom, may as well be a normal reaction of a child in a certain circumstance. Also, you must consider the fact that it can be especially difficult to control a child's diet. If your child goes to school this will add to the torment, because in a collective he will be exposed to foods that are forbidden, and refusal to eat them may led to exclusion from the group. You must realize that many children and young adults are already "addicted" on foods containing preservatives, colorants and massive amounts of sugar and the transition will be hard, but not impossible.

There are children who realize that they have a problem and they want to fix it. In this case, things are easier as they are more than willing to cooperate, and even read labels to avoid what makes them misbehave.

Regardless of the impediments along the way or the problems that arise from changing your child's diet and lifestyle, it is definitely something any parent should try, it's cheaper and much safer than using stimulant drugs, and if your child doesn't have a healthy diet now, this may improve the overall state of health, and may also be more nutritious.

The worst case scenario is that the modified diet won't do anything and you can then try other options.

You should always keep track and try to do so, while being objective. Use a notebook or a chart, even the computer. Write down the ADHD behavior your child exhibits, do so before beginning the diet and during. Ask the people that interact with your child, teachers, friends, baby sitter, grandparents, if they've noticed changes in his behavior. Don't tell them that you've done something to improve their ADHD, this will influence their response. Write all the new information in your chart. Also, you should keep a diet diary too, this way; when you correlate the two it will help you understand what foods worsen the symptoms.

There are quite a few diets out there and the amount of information can be confusing but the basic idea is exclusion of factors that lead to bad behaviors.

One of the most popular diets is the Feingold diet which is based on eliminating additives and foods that contain salicylates, including aspirin. Salicylates are natural pesticide that plants make to protect themselves and are found in: Apples, apricots, grapes and raisins, plums and prunes, oranges, peaches and nectarines, almonds and also in tomatoes, cucumbers and pickles.

The diet also eliminates:

Artificial dyes, for this you must read the labels carefully, the aliments must not contain "Red 40" and "Yellow 5" but other colorants should be avoided too. Some food dyes are made from petroleum, and this is the same compound that makes gasoline.

Artificial flavorings, sadly this includes Synthetic vanilla; artificial flavorings can be made from many chemicals and companies can use any mix they choose. Synthetic vanilla is the waste product of paper mills.

Artificial sweeteners, the most common in this category are "aspartame", "Sucralose" and "Acesulfame-K".

Preservatives like BHA, BHT and TBHQ, this particular category requires more attention because, sometimes, they are listed on the label as "anti-oxidants" because they don't allow fats to become rancid. Natural anti-oxidants are healthy, but these certainly don't fall in that category. Some other food additives that you want to avoid would be: sodium benzoate, nitrites and sulfites.

The hard part is that these ingredients must be eliminated completely, and people don't usually realize how much of our food is "infested". Preservatives aren't found just in cookies, soda and candy, they are everywhere in the cereals that we eat in the morning, in the fries from the restaurant next door, and even in the "natural juice" we buy from the supermarket.

If you place your child on this diet, he will be able to eat everything else, but you must make sure that he doesn't snack elsewhere.

Chapter 14: Honing In On My Child's Abilities

Before you can understand your child's strengths and weaknesses, you must first understand what normal behavior is for a child. It is true that all children are different, but there is a standard spectrum of age-appropriate behavior that all children should meet. While your child does not need to be in the very top of the scale, they should fall somewhere in the range in order to be considered as progressing normally.

Up until now, ADHD has been identified and responded to base on reactions to the symptoms that each child has. Now that we have a better understanding of what's involved we can better come up with a course of treatment that will benefit both child and adult and help them to better navigate the ups and downs of the problem.

Executive Skills

A term you will need to become familiar with is that of executive skills. Most people will view this term in relation to being able to perform certain executive tasks like running a business or organizational skills. However, this is not the true meaning when it comes to ADHD. While the ability to plan, decide, and perform tasks is definitely a part of it, the focus should be on the word 'executive.' It is the ability to 'execute' those things you planned, decided upon, and want to do.

Every person needs executive skills in their daily lives whether they are conducting a business or not. Even the simplest of tasks require these types of skills. Think about a simple task you might ask your child to do, eating all their food on the plate. To you, it may be a pretty straightforward thing to do but to the child it involves...

Choosing the right utensil to use

Utilizing that utensil in the right way.

Deciding which item of food to put in the mouth first

Chewing the food

And returning to pick up another item of food.

In normal children, this is usually done without much fanfare, but the ADHD child may see something exciting in the shape of the food and rather than eating it may discover a number of ways to play with it instead. They may lose interest in chewing and swallowing and prefer to spit or throw the food offending others around them. Even if the child is able to function well at the dinner table, there are many other decisions that may affect his behavior. The relationship he has with his siblings, the number of other distractions in the room, and the risk-reward ratio all are part of the process.

A child without ADHD makes a normal progression towards adulthood with little or no problem, but the ADHD child may struggle with this process every step of the way. Every decision becomes a chore from what foods to eat to something as simple and normal as knowing how to comb their own hair and could present a potential minefield. The development of this skill is a gradual process, and it is reasonable to expect that a child will reach a relative semi-adult independence by the time they reach their late adolescent years. However, they will still need to be reminded occasionally as they progress towards adulthood at which point your primary parenting role will reach its end. None of this is possible for the child if he has not yet mastered these executive skills.

Of course, there are several different types of executive skills that a child must develop. These can be viewed from two different perspectives. First, we can look at them from the developmental angle, these are progressive in nature. In other words, the natural order in which children their age learn these skills. You can also view them from a fundamental perspective; in other words in recognizing what they help the child to do.

Likely the easiest way to understand them is from the developmental perspective. Most people recognize and understand the abilities natural to a toddler, a kindergartener, or a primary school aged child. When you know the order in which certain skills are expected in each child, you can more easily identify if your child is falling low on the spectrum. Let's look at each of these skills and how they develop in the average child.

Response Inhibition: The ability to think before acting

Children who have mastered response inhibition are able to make the connection between stimulus from their environment and the associated rewards. In other words, they learn to respond to stimuli according to an expected result. It is a normal response to both humans and animals. However, those with ADHD struggle to maintain control over their actions and often react without thinking without regard to what the consequences are.

Young children are usually able to wait for a short amount of time without getting overly anxious or disruptive while older children are capable of hearing a decision from an authority figure without debating the issue or becoming argumentative.

Working Memory

This is the ability to recall information and connect it to present tasks. It involves bringing past experiences to mind and applying them to current situations. As a child gets older, they should be able to complete more and more complex tasks. A young child may be only able to complete a one or two step task using their working memory, but an older child should be capable of recalling instructions given to them by a number of different people.

Emotional Control

The ability to control emotions while working on certain tasks or waiting for expectations to be fulfilled is difficult for any child. Non-ADHD children usually master this skill and can handle disappointment at a very early age. Teenagers often have to handle all sorts of emotions as they navigate between test taking, heavy homework assignments, and a variety of stress-related incidents in their daily lives and can still manage to get their tasks done.

Sustained Attention Span

Normally progressive children have the capacity to not only pay attention but are also able to extend their attention span for progressively longer periods of time as they age without getting bored or distracted. Younger children should be able to do this for at least five minutes while teenagers should be able to hold their attention for at least one to two hours.

Task Initiation

Children have the ability to get started on a project within a reasonable amount of time without procrastinating. Younger children should be able to start as soon as instructions are given and teenagers should be able to choose a time to start without waiting until the very last minute.

Prioritizing/Creating a Plan of Action

The ability to create a step-by-step plan of action from start to finish on an assignment or a task. This skill also involves decision making in the process. The child must be able to choose which steps are more important and be able to prioritize them in proper order. Younger children should be able to find ways to resolve issues with their peers while teenagers should be able to develop bigger plans for choosing a university or applying for a job without minimal help.

Organization

The ability to create a system to keep their things in order early on. Young children, with a little coaching, should be able to figure out how to organize their room, school supplies, and playthings. Teenagers should be able to organize their things on their own without any coaching from parents or other adults.

Time Management

Time Management is the ability to determine the best way to make use of their time. It involves understanding how much time they have to accomplish a certain task and find ways to make the best use of it. To accomplish this, they must view time as important and something that should be respected. Younger children should be able to follow schedules and time limits set by adults, but older children and teenagers should be able to create their own schedules to manage the tasks they have to do.

Goal-Directed Persistence

The ability to establish a specific goal and to stay on task until its completion without getting distracted or drawn into more appealing projects. Young children should be able to see small rewards as a powerful enough goal to persist in a project while teenagers should be able to work on a job for a day, a week or more to earn enough money to buy an object of interest.

Flexibility

The ability to adjust their schedules, expectations, and behaviors in the face of changes, obstacles, or other challenges in order to get their job done. Younger children should be able to adjust to changes and obstacles with little disappointment while teenagers should be expected to reasonably adjust their tasks when they are not able to get their first option without fuss.

Metacognition

Every child must be able to stand back and take an objective view of their situation and determine how best to handle it. This is a self-evaluating skill where they take the role of an outsider, mentally step outside of themselves and observe how they are problem-solving and make adjustments accordingly. Young children should be expected to adjust their behavior after receiving constructive input from an adult while teenagers should be able to analyze his or her own conduct in a situation and make the proper adjustments on their own.

Being able to understand these executive skills is paramount to understanding your child's developmental progress. These skills outline the very basic progress that every child should make and while it may not happen at the same time for each child, if your children's peers are steadily picking up these skills and your child is languishing behind the pack it is cause for concern.

Studies have shown that some of these skills happen as early as the first year of a child's life. For example, response inhibition, working memory, and emotional control seem to occur somewhere between the child's first six to twelve months of life. The planning stage develops soon after. You may not readily observe these skills as they develop but you see them when your child begins to communicate to you his needs and wants. He may not be able to speak yet but has learned to communicate, he develops strategies on how he will get you to understand he needs to be fed, he wants his blankie or if he needs changing.

In the second year, children develop other skills like flexibility, time management, and task initiation. They may appear as very simple forms at first but will become progressively more refined as the child ages. Once you recognize that your child is not keeping up with the other children his age you have a decision to make. ADHD comes in two different forms. Depending on which skills they are weak in the child is not able to either **think** correctly or your child is not able to **behave** correctly.

As you analyze your child using these skills as a measure, you can determine exactly what she needs to get back on track. For example, if his weakness is in an area where he is struggling to recall instructions then you can direct your efforts to create strategies that will help him to retrieve those memories when he needs them. If the weakness is managing emotions, then you will find strategies that will give him tools for those areas.

While both types of skills are necessary for development, thinking skills are used to set goals and create the plans of action needed to achieve them. They help them to be self-seekers, finding their own way to getting what they want or need. However, thinking skills can only take your child so far. They will never be able to achieve their goals if they cannot implement the **behavior** skills. A good plan is only that if the child cannot exercise initiative to get started or maintain sustainability to see it through to the end. The two actually work in tandem, one can only do so much, so your child also needs to be able to master both sets of executive skills in order to succeed.

Now that you know these executive skills you should be able to see them as they grow in your child. It is perfectly normal for a baby to feed from a bottle during their formative years but one would think it quite strange if they were still using a bottle by the time they were in school. It is the exact same things with these executive skills. Their impact on your child may not be as obvious as sucking on a bottle, but they are just as important to your child's developing maturity as he grows older.

These executive skills are the key factors used by medical and psychological professionals to determine if a child actually does have ADHD. While you may consult with your doctor about this concern the chances are that parents have already observed these gaps in executive skills and have a pretty good idea that their child has ADHD even before the consultation.

While many may disagree on the degree of absence of these skills, they all seem to have a general consensus that if these skills are lacking, then it is a case of ADHD. Primary skills they focus on are response inhibition, sustained attention, time management, task management, goal-directed persistence and working memory. These are usually the highest indicators of the disorder. Other skills may also be lacking, but these are the ones that are noticed first. If parents have not recognized them then likely they are pointed out to them by their child's teachers and other adults their child may need to interact with.

It is true that the development of these skills can be slow in many children, even those without ADHD. We have even seen some adults that struggle to keep track of their things are always misplacing their keys, or have a hard time focusing on things that are of no interest to them. These weakness actually to some degree are a part of all of us. However, if you witness a child with a string of these skills lagging behind other children or they do not seem to be growing out of them then it is time to do something about it. Others may tell you that it is not important, to just buckle down and get tough or some other cliché that implies that it's something else, but you owe it to yourself and to your child to make sure that they get all the help they need as early as possible so they can mature in a way that ensures their self-esteem remains intact.

Chapter 15: What Is Adhd?

Attention Deficit Hyperactivity Disorder or ADHD is a developmental neuropsychiatric disorder, in which there are significant problems with a person's executive functions, like attentional and inhibitory control, that may cause attention deficits, hyperactivity, or impulsiveness, which is not appropriate for a person's age.

This disorder is very common to school-aged children, a period where children are very active and adventurous, which often makes it hard for parents to distinguish the symptoms of the disorder. It is also three-times more common to boys than girls for an unknown reason. It is hard to diagnose. Even though it is the most common childhood disorder, it can continue through adolescence and adulthood.

ADHD is hard to identify because unlike other psychological disorder, it doesn't have a standardized test that you can use to know if one of your loved ones do have

ADHD. Additionally, ADHD's symptoms, especially to the children are hard to diagnose because most of the symptoms are similar to kids attitude.

Children with ADHD often act without thinking, which makes them have a hard time following rules and instructions. It is also hard for them to focus on a specific thing or task, and tend to find other things or activities that interest them more.

They know how to listen to instructions and are usually aware of the expectations to them by the people around, but it still very difficult for them to accomplish tasks due to having trouble on focusing to details and paying attention.

Given that children are usually very active and do not focus on things, the difference between a normal kid from a child that has ADHD, can be determined through symptoms.

A child diagnosed with ADHD, has the tendency of having their symptoms for a longer period of time which often occurs, compared to those who are normal. These symptoms affect children's social outlook, which makes it hard for them to get along with other children normally. It also affects the academic functions of a child that gives them the feeling that they are different from the rest of the class.

Chapter 16: What Is Adhd?

ADHD stands for attention deficit hyperactivity disorder. It is a medical condition. A person with ADHD has differences in brain development and brain activity that affect attention, the ability to sit still, and self-control. ADHD can affect a child at school, at home, and in friendships.

Attention deficit hyperactivity disorder (ADHD) affects children and teens and can continue into adulthood. ADHD is the most commonly diagnosed mental disorder of children.

Children with ADHD may be hyperactive and unable control their impulses. Or they may have trouble paying attention. These behaviors interfere with school and home life.

It's more common in boys than in girls. It's usually discovered during the early school years, when a child begins to have problems paying attention.

Adults with ADHD may have trouble managing time, being organized, setting goals, and holding down a job. They may also have problems with relationships, self-esteem, and addiction.

FALSE ORGIN OF ADHD

There are a number of myths about the origins of ADHD. In past decades, there was a prevalent theory that certain foods and sugar can increase the risk of developing the condition. However, researchers are doubtful that there is any connection between these substances and children's behaviors and ability to learn.

Research has also disproven the ideas that hormones or the vestibular system (the part of the brain that affects balance) are related to hyperactivity or ADHD.

Perhaps the most common myth is that ADHD is caused by poor parenting or a difficult family environment. Lack of discipline or too much television, video games, or Internet use can be blamed for the condition.

Though environmental factors such as parenting style and stressors in the family can influence the severity of symptoms and the level of impairment, they do not cause ADHD.

Rather than blame themselves for their child's hyperactivity and impulsivity, parents can focus instead on how they can best help their child get the help they need. When you practice objectivity about the origins of a condition, your free yourself to make smart and healthy choices for yourself and your family. How can you help your child today to get the best support for their ADHD?

CAUSES OF ADHD

Attention Deficit Hyperactivity Disorder is a chronic condition that affects a person's level of hyperactivity and impulse control. ADHD influences the parts of the brain that help us with what is known as executive functioning.

This includes problem solving, planning for the future, evaluating behaviors, regulating emotions, and controlling our impulses.

When ADHD causes challenges in a family, a classroom, or a workplace, people can become quick to lose sight of the facts. Parents might worry if they did something wrong in raising their child.

They may assume that they used the wrong parenting methods or that an early stressful event in a child's life caused the condition.

Teachers might dismiss a student as lazy or disobedient. Spouses might see their partner as unconcerned about their own needs or emotions. The first step in helping a person with ADHD understands the origins of the condition. By understanding that these origins typically include genetic factors, people can become more objective about the condition and its effects, and blame doesn't have to be placed on parents or the person with ADHD.

ADHD and Heredity

Genetics studies are just beginning to identity genes associated with ADHD. In addition to molecular genetic research, the hereditary component of the condition has been supported by various family studies. For example, one study found that over 25% of relatives of families with a child with ADHD also had the condition, a much higher rate than in families without a child with ADHD.

Also, twin studies have demonstrated that there is an 82% chance that identical twins will both have ADHD if at least one of them has the condition, compared to a 38% chance among fraternal twins.

Finally, children with ADHD who were adopted are more likely to have ADHD present in their biological families than in their adopted families. This confirms that the genetic component is much stronger than any environmental factors.

ADHD and Other Factors

Though the genetic component is considered to be the main cause of ADHD, other environmental and situation factors have been examined as potential contributors. For example, research has noted a correlation between women who use cigarettes and/or consume alcohol while pregnant and the risk of their child developing ADHD. High lead levels among preschool-aged children may also contribute to the development of the condition, so kids who live in older buildings may be at risk.

Brain injury from a traumatic event such as a stroke, tumor, or blow to the head can also produce symptoms of inattention and impulsivity that are similar to ADHD, but only a very small percentage of children with an ADHD diagnosis have suffered any brain trauma.

ADHD IN GIRLS AND WOMEN

ADHD in girls and women is often difficult to detect. For many years, attention deficit hyperactivity disorder (ADHD) was thought to be a condition experienced solely by boys.

While boys are more likely to be given an ADHD diagnosis, it's not because girls are necessarily at lower risk for the disorder. They just sometimes exhibit symptoms that don't adhere to the traditional ideas and images people historically have about ADHD. This makes them less likely to be referred for mental health services as well.[1]

Girls with ADHD

When thinking of ADHD, many people imagine a child who can't sit still and acts impulsively, blurting out answers in class or interrupting their parents. But many girls with ADHD may be sitting quietly, seemingly daydreaming and struggling to finish a task or organize their lives.

These subtler symptoms make the disorder often go unnoticed, with many females not receiving an official diagnosis until they reach adulthood.

Other common signs of ADHD in girls can include:

Wandering thoughts

Trouble finishing projects and schoolwork

Being late often

Difficulty concentrating

A disorganized room or workspace

Getting upset easily

Girls and women can also exhibit symptoms of hyperactivity of impulsivity. Girls with ADHD can be highly physically active, taking risks as they play, or they might be extremely talkative, excitable, and emotional.

40% of girls, however, will outgrow symptoms of hyperactivity and impulsivity by the time they reach adulthood.

Risk for Co-occurring Disorders

Many girls with ADHD may feel capable of managing symptoms when they are in elementary school, but the extracurricular, social, and increased academic demands of middle school and high school may cause them to struggle.

Girls also may be more likely to blame themselves for their symptoms, labeling themselves as incapable of doing well or being "stupid." This inward focus puts them at higher risk for major depression, anxiety disorders, and eating disorders than girls who do not have ADHD.

One study found that girls with combined-type ADHD (having symptoms of both inattention and hyperactivity) are at high risk for suicide and self-harm.

Women with ADHD

Many women are first diagnosed with ADHD in adulthood, and they may seek treatment because they struggle to manage the demands of work, home, and daily life.

They struggle with executive functioning and to complete tasks that require organization, planning, and time management. Struggling to keep up, they put themselves at risk for depression, decreased self-esteem, substance abuse, sleep problems, and overeating.

In addition to medication, females with ADHD can also benefit from therapeutic interventions such as building self-esteem, promoting healthy habits, learning time management, and practicing stress-management techniques.

Family therapy can help educate family members about the diagnosis and teach them to problem-solve together and communicate better. Peer support groups can also help women feel less shame about their symptoms and feel empowered to gain control over their daily lives and futures.

Action Steps

Ask for Help – ADHD is highly treatable in both men and women of all ages, with medication, behavioral therapy, or a combination of the two often combatting symptoms very effectively.

Don't be discouraged if the first medication or intervention isn't an exact fit (for you or your daughter), and keep talking to your doctor or a mental health professional about concerns and successes. Be sure to tell the doctor about other medical conditions and mental health history to help guide medication and therapy recommendations.

Praise Progress – Take the time to notice progress and improvement in your daughter's daily life, no matter how small. Being able to see setbacks as functions of the condition rather than a personal failing and to take pride in successes can lower the risk of depression and help your child gain a stronger sense of control over their health and their future. Starting treatment in childhood can have a huge impact on future outcomes and functioning, so practice optimism about the condition.

Know Your Rights – If your school-age child is severely impacted by her ADHD, she may qualify for an Individualized Education Program (IEP), or a 504 Plan, and extra educational supports.

Even if a child does not qualify, talk to school staff about how teachers, school counselors, and other staff can support your daughter as she prepares to thrive in an academic environment. School personnel may also subscribe to stereotypes about ADHD and need education about what symptoms they should monitor in your child's daily performance.

Find Mentors – All of us, and especially children, can benefit from examples of people who have overcome challenges or adversity. If you know a woman or teenager who has successfully managed the symptoms of her ADHD, considering asking them to connect with your daughter. Being able to visualize success can encourage her progress and decrease the risk of low self-esteem or negative labeling.

ADULT ADHD

Attention Deficit Hyperactivity Disorder is a chronic condition that affects a person's level of hyperactivity and impulse control. Adults can be diagnosed with ADHD, though symptoms typically emerge when they are children. When symptoms are left untreated, they can cause problems for adults at work and school and in relationships.

Sixty percent of children who have ADHD will experience the disorder as adults. In the United States, that's roughly 8 million adults. However, less than 20% of those adults will be diagnosed and treated.1 Signs of ADHD in adults can sometimes be more difficult to spot than in children.

They might be less hyperactive than a child with the diagnosis, but deep down they are struggling with paying attention, staying on task, and warding off impulsive behaviors. Many adults might not realize that forgetting plans, prioritizing their to-do list, and feeling impatient and moody might be signs of a treatable condition.

Adult ADHD Symptoms

Trouble focusing on a task

Feelings of restlessness

Organization problems

Feeling easily frustrated

Poor time management

Impulsive decision-making

Experiencing mood swings

Poor coping skills for stress

These symptoms can cause problems in multiple areas of life.2 An adult with untreated ADHD might struggle with school or maintaining steady employment. Impulsive behaviors may lead to legal issues, accidents, drug or alcohol abuse, or poor physical health. Mood swings and trouble focusing can also cause relationship problems with family, friends, and partners. The weight of these issues can also lead to low self-esteem, particularly when a person labels themselves as being "lazy."

Chapter 17: Understanding Adhd

Attention Deficit Hyperactivity Disorder, or ADHD for short, is a common condition that affects millions of children worldwide. ADHD is also known as ADD (Attention Deficit Disorder), though the latter is an outdated term. According to the Centers for Disease Control and Prevention, approximately 6.4 million children in the United States alone suffer from ADHD.

What is ADHD?

ADHD is a chronic condition that begins in childhood, and often persists into adulthood. It is characterized by inattentiveness, hyperactivity, and impulsiveness. Children with ADHD are unable to control their behavior due to the difficulty of processing neural stimuli. ADHD is accompanied by a high level of motor activity, hence the hyperactive characteristic of the disorder.

Often, a child who suffers from ADHD is extremely talkative, unable to sit still, and

150

is easily distracted. He may experience other byproducts of ADHD, such as poor performance, low grades in school, troubled relationships, and a decreased self-esteem. In some cases, symptoms of ADHD lessen with age; in other cases, however, symptoms persist regardless of age. Such people can control their ADHD symptoms through strategy and management.

Types of ADHD

ADHD is classified into three distinct subtypes:

Inattentive: In the old days, inattentive ADHD was referred to as ADD. Children with this type of ADHD show more symptoms of inattentiveness than impulsiveness or hyperactivity. A constant inability to focus is usually a telltale sign of Inattentive ADHD. Other symptoms include:

Frequent daydreaming, or "spacing out"

Quickly shifts from task to task without accomplishing anything

151

Misses both important and trivial details

Decreased interest or gets bored easily

Becomes easily distracted

A decreased ability to process and comprehend information

A decreased ability to follow instructions

Extremely forgetful

2. **Hyperactive-Compulsive:** Children with this type of ADHD show symptoms of both hyperactivity and compulsiveness, but not inattentiveness. Other symptoms of Hyperactive-Compulsive ADHD include:

Fidgeting, or an inability to sit still

Excessive talking

Has difficulty doing quiet tasks such as reading and drawing

Continuous running around from place to place

An urge to touch everything he can get his hands on

Purposely running into people or objects

Constant jumping and climbing

Frequently interrupting conversations

Impatience

Combined: Children with the combined type of ADHD have the qualities of inattentiveness, impulsiveness, and hyperactivity.

Normal Behavior vs. ADHD

Most, if not all, children are energetic, impulsive, inattentive, and a little hyper at times. School-age children naturally have short attention spans and a low level of interest in particular subjects. These children should not be written off as having ADHD, as some children simply have a higher activity level than others. If a child's performance and relationships at home or school remain unaffected, it's not likely that he has ADHD. However, if a child has problems at school, is often in trouble, and shows abnormally high levels of energy and activity, then it may be wise to see a doctor.

ADHD Severity

ADHD cases vary in both nature and severity. Symptoms may be mild, moderate, or severe depending on the child's environment and unique physiology. Some children, for instance, experience moderate inattentiveness when tasked with unfavorable chores. Those same children, however, may not have any issues with inattention when asked do tasks they enjoy. ADHD symptoms may become severe during group situations that are unstructured such as in the cafeteria or on the playground. This increase in severity is due to the lack of structure that the child is accustomed to in the classroom where rewards tend to be given.

Causes of ADHD

The exact causes of ADHD aren't clear. However, researchers believe that genetics play a key role. A child is more susceptible to developing ADHD if he has a family history of the disorder. Being born premature and having a low birth weight are also connected to ADHD.

Environmental factors may increase a child's risk for ADHD as well. Factors that contribute to ADHD include:

Diet: Children and adolescents who consume a high intake of sodium, saturated fats, and refined sugars are twice as likely to be diagnosed with ADHD. A deficiency in essential omega-3 fatty acids also appear to contribute to ADHD.

2.**Chemical Exposure:** Certain chemicals used in manufacturing products are strongly linked with ADHD. Industrial compounds like PFCs used in food packaging and chemicals such as phthalates, which are found in some toys, are just a few examples of ADHD-inducing chemicals.

3.**Head or Brain Injuries:** Children who have suffered from brain trauma as a result of disease, a brain tumor, or a severe blow to the head may exhibit symptoms of ADHD. Brain injuries are closely linked with inattention, impulsivity, and hyperactivity.

4.Pesticides: Children who consume produce sprayed with pesticides are likely to be diagnosed with ADHD. To reduce the risk, it is advisable to purchase organic varieties of fruits and vegetables.

5.Smoking and Drinking During Pregnancy: Exposing an unborn child to tobacco and alcohol increases his risk for having ADHD. Fetal exposure to alcohol can cause fetal alcohol syndrome, the symptoms of which, are similar to ADHD symptoms.

6.Lead Exposure: Lead is a neurotoxin, and exposure to it is harmful to brain tissue— particularly in developing tissue. Lead affects the behavior of children who are exposed to lead in early childhood.

7. **Food Additives:** Certain preservatives and artificial food colors may increase a young child's risk for becoming hyperactive. You don't have to put your child on a diet, or ban brightly colored foods; but it would be smart to reduce consumption of processed and colored

foods if your child is already at risk for ADHD.

8.TV or Video Games: Research has found a correlation between attention problems and time spent watching TV or playing video games. School-age children who spend too much time in front of a TV screen have more attention issues than those who don't.

Tests and Diagnosis

If your child is exhibiting more than six symptoms of ADHD, it may be time to talk to a doctor. The doctor will most likely conduct a series of tests to rule out other medical conditions that may be causing the symptoms. Conditions with similar symptoms include anxiety, depression, earning disabilities, and sleep apnea.

The following matters all produce ADHD-like symptoms, and will need to be ruled out by a doctor for proper diagnosis:

Giftedness: Inattention may result when a child is gifted by nature. He may be bored with the topics being taught in the classroom if he does not feel challenged.

2.**Abuse:** Abuse or neglect could lead to emotional problems that are unrelated to ADHD. Behavioral issues are often linked to abusive conditions.

3.**Malnutrition:** When a young child is not getting the essential vitamins and nutrients needed for mental and physical sustenance, it may result in compromised brain development.

4.**Stressful Home Environment:** Trauma that results from a divorce or the death of a loved one may cause a child to exhibit uncharacteristic behavior such as loss of interest and an inability to focus in school.

The diagnosis will be based on an interview with the child, an analysis of his or her medical history, a review of family medical history, behavior rating scales, and a physical exam.

In addition to ruling out other conditions and exhibiting symptoms, a child must meet the following additional criteria to be diagnosed with ADHD:

He exhibits ADHD symptoms before the age of 12.

He exhibits ADHD symptoms in at least two settings—home, school, at the store, at church, with friends, etc.

Clear evidence that the symptoms interfere with performance at school and relationships.

The symptoms are not explained by any other health condition or personal matter.

Adult ADHD

Typically, adults who suffer from ADHD have had the disorder since childhood. Sometimes, ADHD goes unnoticed, and remains undiagnosed until later on in life. Many children outgrow ADHD while others have it for life. Like children, adults can be diagnosed with any of the three types of ADHD. Adults manage ADHD symptoms more readily than children due to their maturity and physical differences. Most simply learn to adapt to their condition.

Symptoms

Inability to meet deadlines

Difficulty organizing tasks

Poor concentration skills

Difficulty remembering information

Difficulty following directions

Challenges

Adults with ADHD often face challenges in many aspects of life due to their symptoms. They may have trouble with:

Depression

Impulsiveness

Anxiety

Chronic boredom

Chronic forgetfulness

Problems at work, home, or school

Bad temper

Mood swings

Lack of organizational skills

Low self-esteem

Alcohol abuse

Drug addiction

Relationship problems

Marital problems

Chapter 18: My Child Has Been Diagnosed With Adhd. What's Next?

Parents who have just been given the diagnosis that their child has ADHD get very confused and has a lot of questions, concerns and they sometimes deny the diagnosis.

Your child has been diagnosed with ADHD. It may be a relief in some ways, to put a name with the issues you have been dealing with. One decision parents have to contemplate, which is rather large a decision, is whether to medicate or not medicate their child who is struggling with ADHD. There is no right or wrong answer. The decision to medicate or not needs to be addressed on an individual basis by the family and caretakers.

You need to talk this over with your significant other, family members, caretakers etc. You may also want to talk to other parents that you know who may have children or know someone that may have children with ADHD to get their input. The bottom line is only you can make that decision.

There are times when you may need to start your child off with medication while looking for alternative treatments if that is your goal. If your child had diabetes would you not him/her medications to control their diabetes.

There are several treatment options to choose from therefore parents, doctors, therapists, counselors and other caregivers should work together for the benefit of the child. You are your child's advocate so make use of all the resources available to you and your child.

Parents should attend a parental training course which will help them to deal with issues that will arise from their child's behavior.

A good treatment plan will include close monitoring of the child with follow ups and any changes that may be needed.

Treatment options for ADHD

Medications

Alternative therapy

Behavioral interventions

Education

Nature

Swimming

Education

Nature

Swimming

Transformation Program

The decision to medicate or not medicate your child is a difficult one that you really have to think about.

If you choose to medicate your child have the doctor who is prescribing medications to let you know how the medication will affect your child. Any symptoms of drowsiness, poor appetite, difficulty in sleeping or eating if there are feeling nauseated and any other side effects that you should look for. How long the child should be on the medication before seeing any improvement. How long they may need to be on the medication.

Children tolerate medications differently so what may work for one child may not work for another. Sometimes the side effects of these medications such as Ritalin, Dexedrine and others may be worse than the child actual ADHD.

Getting the most from the education system:

Can My Child Be Given Medications at School?

Yes! Your child is allowed to take medications at school but a special form called a 504 form has to be completed by the doctor and then taken to the school nurse with the medications. The nurse will have the child come down to the nurse's office at the appropriate time to take their medication.

This plan needs to be included in the child Individualized Education Program (IEP.)

Need to maintain the child and parents right to confidentiality.

Medications are to be administered in accordance with the rules of the facility.

We will discuss alternative therapies in more detail later on.

Behavioral therapy

Behavior therapy does help many children, but there must be clarity consistency and persistence for it to work. Do not expect results overnight, this may be a long process but all care givers have to chip in and help.

Make sure the child understands what you say to him/her, you can also have your child repeat what you just said to make sure they understand the instructions that were given.

There should be consequences for appropriate and inappropriate behaviors. The child should understand which behaviors are acceptable and which are not. The behaviors you want to change in your child should be written down and put where the child can see it.

Do not try to change all the behaviors at the same time. Just work on one or two of the most important ones. If you try to make too many changes at the same time the child may become confused and frustrated and it will not work.

Education

Most children start school in regular classes. Many parents do not know that there is a problem with their child until they start school. If the teacher finds there is a problem they will call the parents to let them know their child has not been paying attention, constantly moving around when they should be sitting, blurting out answers, difficulty focusing, daydreaming etc.

With the classes in most schools with over 30 children to teach most teachers put pressure on parents to have their child seen by their doctor to either put them on medications to calm them in the class room or to rule out ADHD. With such large classes the teachers find it impossible to deal with these children and teach at the same time because some of these children are very disruptive.

Most children do not do well in the education system because they need extra attention and disrupt the class. A lot of parents home school their children because the child cannot keep up with the work at school.

If you think your child has a problem with hyperactivity or attention or having a problem with learning you can request the school to perform an assessment for your child. Schools are required to perform this assessment if you request it. This is a free service performed by the school.

You can choose whether your child goes to a public school, private school or whether you home school your child. If you have placed your child in a private school, or if your child's school does not receive federal funding, you may not have access to many of the services and accommodations offered in public schools.

Parents can relate to those who are doing the assessment the type of educational difficulties their child is having.

The school cannot make a diagnosis only a trained health professional can diagnose a child.

The child has to be accurately diagnosed by a knowledgeable well trained clinician. Most parents fear the word ADHD and go into denial. With the proper diagnosis there is a lot of help you can find for your child.

The doctor may want to try your child on medications; several different medications may need to be tried before finding one that will actually help your child. So you need to be very patient.

Should your child need to take medications during school hours a special form is filled out (a form called 504) and has to be signed by the doctor so the child can be given their medications during school hours.

The child may also be assigned to a special education class in which they are taught their lessons in a much smaller classroom setting. This way the child can get individual attention and work at a pace that is comfortable for him/her.

For children who are younger than 5 years old you may want to contact Early Childhood Programs that are specialized with helping the little ones with disabilities.

These children learn best in a structure environment whether at home or at school. The rules and expectations should be clear and consistent ahead of time and consequences delivered immediately.

The rules and regulations should be explained in simple terms that the child can understand using short sentences and having the child repeat what was just said so they understand.

Accommodations for helping the child

The following may be helpful:

Speak short sentences so the child understands and have them repeat what you just said.

Setting specific times for specific tasks, these children do not deal with changes too well. They need a routine.

When you have to change anything from their routine let them know ahead of time.

Make a daily schedule with any assignments.

Have a quiet space for the child to work.

Have them sit at the front of the class where there is less distraction away from doors and windows.

Provide frequent breaks.

They may want to stand or sit on the floor to do their class work because they feel more comfortable that way.

Using visual instructions instead of verbal instructions.

Using computer for learning.

Need to be taught organizational skills.

Modifying test time.

Chapter 19: Other Mental Health Conditions

Associated with ADHD

There are тeveral conditionт that are associated with ADHD, including anxiety, learning diтabilitieт, oppoтitional defiant diтorder, тubтtance abuтe, biopolar diтorder,25 depreттion, and тocial anxiety. Thiт iт why it'т critical that an ADHD evaluation also include an initial aттeттment for theтe related conditionт, aт well aт ongoing тcreeningт if an ADHD diagnoтiт iт made. If one of theтe related conditionт iт alтo diagnoтed, the doctor can recommend a number of treatments optionт that, similar to ADHD, will include medication and therapy.

Living with ADHD

A child or adult diagnoтed with ADHD faceт daily challenges that impact nearly every area of hiт or her life. But perтiттence in finding the right medication and doтage while alтo making time for therapy that focuses on effective behavioral coping techniqueт will be the key to тuccетtfully managing this condition.

33 CBD Oil

Cannabidiol, or CBD, iт one of the active cannabinoids in cannabiт. It can actually account for up to 40% of the active cannabinoid content.

CBD hemp oil iт made from hemp that has high amounts of CBD

and low amountт of THC. THC is the cannabinoid that moтt people are familiar with. It iт responsible for the "high" that you get if you take or smoke marijuana.

Thiт meanт that CBD oil iт non-pтychoactive. This has allowed CBD oil to be uтed for a lot of medical purpoтeт because you don't have to worry about it affecting your mental state.

I don't know about you, but even if тomething waт really

helpful, I wouldn't be able to function at all if I was ттoned all day and night.

174

CBD Oil Dosage

we've got the dosage topic covered but you тhould alwayт

consult with your doctor before beginning any form of treatment. CBD-rich oil comeт in a variety of concentrationт and forms, and while moтt bottles come with a user manual, CBD oil 34

works differently for each perтon. If you've never tried CBD or you are тtill trying to figure out what workт beтt for you, then continue reading aт there are a few important things to

understand about CBD oil and CBD oil doтageт.

Important Things to Know About CBD

Oil Dosages

1) Every Perтon iт Different and May Require a Different Doтage

If you've been following the articleт on our site, then you have

probably heard of the endocannabinoid system. Thiт is a unique тyттem in our body that'т reтponтible for improving and maintaining our mental and physical health. CBD iт believed to help regulate that system by binding with various receptorт

located within cell and tiттue systems. Those receptors are referred to aт CB1 and CB2.

The endocannabinoid тyттem is extremely complex and far from underттood, leaving reтearcherт trying to determine whether or not the CBD directly or indirectly effectт thoтe receptorт, and exactly what role they play in affecting ones' health.

35 While the exact way they effect our system ттill remains a mystery to moтт reтearcherт, what we do know is that every

perтon has a different endocannabinoid тyттem, and therefore

while the inттructionт on a CBD oilт' bottle may be informative and clear, the ттandard dosing may affect two different people in completely different ways.

2) Geneticт, Tolerance and General Health

If you accept the fact that everyone iт different, then you can underттand that everyone haт his/her own geneticт, tolerance, and general health. There are thoтe that suffer from тevere

debilitating conditionт and others that are only looking to cure

their day to day anxiety. Each perтon has their own reaтonт for wanting to take CBD oil, and it'т assumed that all of these factorт – geneticт, tolerance and general health – will come into

play aт far aт how well CBD workт for them. It cannot be

expected that тomeone who iт in the prime of their game, from a health perspective, will require the тame dosage aт тomeone

who has severe medical iттueт.

36 3) It'т Not a Miracle Cure

Regardless of whether the right dosage of CBD will work for your body or not, it'т important to underттand that CBD oil is not a miracle cure. Don't expect to take a few drops and, Voilà, you're cured. The effects of CBD oil are not inттant, and people

conттantly make the same miттake – they use CBD for a тhort period, expecting it to cure them inттantly, and when it doeтn't work they complain and aтk for a refund. CBD can take time to

work and тimilar to your health iттueт, it won't happen overnight. The key iт finding the right doтage.

The Standard CBD Oil Dosage Manual

Now, remember, thiт guide iт a general one, and it iт extremely

important to read the dosage instructions on the CBD oil you are taking, especially as results from certain doтageт may affect you differently then otherт. Furthermore, it iт always best to contact the CBD oil company to aтk them the right doтage for your medical condition and conтult with your doctor if required.

With that тaid, there are a few common doтage тtrategieт that might work for you:

37 Start by taking one drop on the first day. It'т important to see how you feel as everyone reactт differently. It may even cause you irritation, and therefore it's important to тtop.

If all goes well, increase the amount to 2 dropт per day for the

firтt 3-4 weekт. This iт the teтting period to тee if it is helping any of your symptoms.

Spread the drops throughout the day. For example, take one in the morning and one in the evening.

If you don't experience any change, then increase at a тlow rate

and тee how you feel. With each person, it iт a question of finding the right dosage.

Remember that many CBD oil companieт adviтe you to put the

drops under your tongue and let them take effect for at least 30

seconds.

Numerous тiteт тtate the following doтage guidelineт when using CBD orally:

☐ General Health: 2.5₁5mg CBD

☐ Chronic pain: 2.5₂0 mg CBD

☐ Sleep diтorderт: 40160 mg CBD

38 CBD Effects and CBD Benefits

CBD oil effects your body by binding to cannabinoid receptors.

You have cannabinoid receptorт all over your body, including your skin and digestive tract.

CBD oil can alтo act aт a 5-HT1 receptor agoniтt, meaning it can help with depreттion and anxiety by playing in a role in the тerotonin pathways.

Becauтe CBD oil affects so many aтpectт of your body, including the endocannabinoid тyттem, it can help with inflammation, mood, memory, immune system, reproduction, pain perception, sleep, and appetite.

The biggest benefits, and why it has gotten so much of the

spotlight lately, is that CBD oil has helped people with rare

conditions such as Dravet syndrome, a rare form of epilepsy that is hard to treat. People have gone from having multiple

seizures per day to being seizure free for an entire week using CBD oil.

One strain of cannabis is called Charlotte's Web, which has

almost no THC in it, and has been used for medical purposes

ever since it helped a girl named Charlotte stop having really bad seizures after trying all the other approaches.

39 CBD oil has clearly proven itself as a therapeutic substance to

help a variety of ailments, and it can alто play a role in helping anxiety and depreттion.

CBD Oil Side Effects

CBD oil can inhibit hepatic drug metabolism and activity of some liver enzymeт, тuch aт cytochrome P450.

One тide effect from taking CBD oil can be having a "dry

mouth", which if you have ever тmoked marijuana, you know what this feels like.

At the current moment, it is unclear aт to whether or not it poтitively or negatively affects people with Parkinтon'т diтeaтe.

However, moтt ттudieт conducted on CBD oil have shown little

to no тide effects. Thiт тpecific review shows that controlled use iт тafe and non-toxic for humans.

I didn't experience any тide effectт when I experimented with CBD oil that had no THC in it.

40 My Personal Experiment and Findings

Using CBD Oil

Here is where CBD oil can get tricky. When I began my journey

into supplementing with CBD to see its potential, I ran into a lot of companies where I had no idea what I was getting.

The quality matters, as it would be easy to market something as

CBD oil when it has very little CBD in it at all.

Some of the products I tried I felt nothing at all even at high doses, others had weird ingredients, and it wasn't until I started experimenting with prescription CBD and high quality brands

that I started to see benefits from it.

I noticed a slight decrease in anxiety and it helped to ease some

of my digestive symptoms. When I took a large amount of the

tincture as an experiment it had a significant calming effect.

Chapter 20: Help Your Child With Adhd Achieve Success Using This Simple Five Strategies

Let's be honest. No matter what your child's medicine is for ADHD, there is no way that these pills are going to teach him to gain the essential skills and strategies through school and family.

This is where a few behavioral strategies are really useful. But I prefer them simple techniques to call to make life easier! You could even call them home management tips or parenting skills. It does not matter what you call them. You just need to get these five strategies on your radar and on the top of the list.

How ADHD friendly is your home?

What is the situation like clutter? Do you know where everything is all the time? Probably not, and that's why areas for school bags, books, clothing, toys set, and so on is so important. First, it saves a lot of time. Second, there is no confusion when everything is in place. Think of the hassle you save. The child will not, even if he or she is haunted by distractions.

So everything is in place. But what about events, meals, bedtimes and so on? If there is no structured routine and everything is done on an "play it by ear" basis, you can not help your child with ADHD at all. Children love routine and love to think they know what happens next. So do adults!

Have a behavior chart in a prominent position?

The best behavior graph is the one with lots of visuals. There are stars and points system performance, good grades and reward positive behavior. I do not advocate long lists of instructions, but to keep things simple.

There will be black points for inappropriate behavior and not to do homework but it is always best to highlight positive behavior.

To give instructions

Sounds simple, right? The problem is that your child's attention span is very short. His or her mind flits around like a butterfly is challenging so even remember what you said ten seconds ago. A great way to keep it nice and simple is the child has to repeat it back to you. No need to go into detail or give additional information or consequences. Keep it short!

Strategies for dealing with distractions

My fourth strategy is all about distractions. But not necessarily to ask your child to keep quiet. Research shows that a secondary physical movement helps the child to focus, so that we can allow them to play with a squeeze ball or fidget toys. Many parents have stability balls, because the act of balancing uses both sides of the brains and it helps the child to focus on the task in hand.

Obviously we are not going to the TV or computer, while listening to background music helps some children to concentrate. It depends on personal taste. Touching screen time in general, it is always wise to limit these and also to prevent over cartoons as attention span and focus will lead to a built up energy after the screentime that is not good.

Help your child to discover his or her strong point

Every child is good at something. ADHD children are often funny, creative and talented in many ways that other children leave jealous. It is time to highlight it and help your child to develop his skills. This is a great way to build confidence and helps the child to forget his other limitations and problems.

By using these five simple strategies, we can really help a child to cope better and make life easier for everyone in the family.

Chapter 21: Effective Conventional Treatment Options And Counseling Methods To Prevent Your Adhd Traits From Decreasing Your Effectiveness

A child affected by attention deficit hyperactivity disorder (ADHD) often becomes a target of fun and even ridicule in a classroom full of normal students. Their physical imperfections set them at a disadvantage. The general reaction of their peers scares them and puts more pressure on them. They need a much more than a helping hand from the teachers and the school.

Medicines

Medicines are prescribed to curb the symptoms of ADHD. The symptoms include hyperactivity, inattention and impulsivity. Medicines and behavior therapies complement each other in the treatment of ADHD children. It is necessary to watch the children carefully when they start on the medicines. The dose has to be right and there is a possibility of the side effects in some patients. In most cases, the severity of the side effects decreases within a few weeks of taking the medicines. The dosage can be modified, if necessary.

Types of medicines

The usual medicines used in the treatment of ADHD are: stimulants, Atomoxetine, clonidine, guanfacine and antidepressants. Stimulants are instrumental in cutting down the hyperactivity and impulsivity and improving the focus. Clonidine and guanfacine treat aggression, inattention and impulsive characteristics.

The medicines must be taken consistently. The effects of the medicines have to be carefully observed and meticulously recorded. In fact, a close observation and an extensive recording of the behavior of the ADHD child form the basis of the treatment of an ADHD patient.

ADHD counseling

Counseling for ADHD includes talking therapies. These encourage the affected children to talk about their problems. These can be useful for the children as also the parents. Discussions give a vent to the pent-up feelings and have a bit of a cathartic effect. They also do a lot of good to the parents. Behavioral therapies usually have a reward system that tempts the ADHD children to curb their symptoms. These back certain actions by promising a small reward for performing that action.

Behavioral therapies

Cognitive behavioral therapy tries to change the thinking and the subsequent actions. Training in social skills puts the child in various roles. The role-play helps them to understand how to behave with others and how their ways affect the others around them. Counselors can also be involved in the individual, small group or large group guidance sessions. They can guide the parents as well as the teachers.

Family education

Family education programs are for the parents of ADHD children. They are taught how to speak with the affected child, how to spend time with the children by playing with them and how to speak or not to speak to them. Specific training programs help the parents to learn ways which will improve the child's behavior and attention span. Sometimes, these courses can be organized both for the child and the parents.

Parental response

The parents have to accept the child as he or she is. They have to realize that the medicines can help only to control the symptoms, not to cure them. They must understand the difference between discipline and punishment when they tackle the child. They must not punish the child because of the failure to curb some behavior. The parents should not cultivate a habit of rejecting every idea of the child. They should respond positively to the good behavior of the child. They should also be able to anticipate some potentially dangerous situations and be able to act early to defuse them.

Group discussions

Group discussions among the parents of ADHD children can produce ideas that can be very helpful in the individual cases. Such gatherings keep coming up with good new ideas and strategies. Some of the ideas are innovative. Each parent can assess these for use at home and can devise a way to control his or her child better. Such groups prove to be an invaluable support in the long. It is not easy for the parents of ADHD child to connect with the parents of normal children. They are often frustrated and experience loneliness. The parent support groups play a very positive role in such situations. Most parents are the victims of such a feeling at least in the initial stage after confirming the ADHD diagnosis in their child.

Behavioral training

The ADHD children have to develop certain skills to be able to listen to something for long. They have to learn to be attentive and to follow the directions.

They need to be trained in various social competencies. If they are trained in these basic skills, they can be more successful in their social and academic life.

The life of ADHD children is not easy. They cannot sit still in a classroom. They cannot concentrate for long. They cannot perform most academic exercises. They find it difficult to complete the homework. This leads to their having a tough time in the class not only the other students, but also with the teachers. What they need is a hand of help, a lot of special attention and regular coaching with patience. They need to be allowed to work at their own pace. The parents, teachers and the school have a special and a more personal role to play in the life of all ADHD children.

Chapter 22: What Is Attention Deficit Hyperactivity Disorder /Adhd?

Attention Deficit Hyperactivity Disorder is a disorder which impacts people of all ages. In the majority of those ADHD, the person has trouble being attentive for long periods, or anything over a few minutes. Other signs of the disorder include Motor restlessness and behavior which can only be described as impulsive. If reports are true, 4 out of every 10 people have ADHD to some degree.

ADHD is a neurobiological (brain) type of disorder. Genes are said to play a major part in many cases. A child will stand a 30% chance of inheriting the disorder if one of his parents or close relatives already has it.

A short time back, researchers believed that ADHD may be caused by bad nutrition. However, nutrition is still thought to be a factor when it comes to the treatment but it is no longer considered the cause.

In a similar fashion, it was thought that factors such as bad parenting, allergies, drugs and head trauma may have been a cause. But again, this is no longer thought to be the case.

Having ADHD

A person living with this disorder is not getting enough neuro chemicals. Or in other words, it means that the brain is not being properly stimulated. Because of this, the brain attempts to discover other ways to get stimulation. Common ways for people with ADHD to stimulate the brain include movements and physical activity. These movements are often involuntary and are a reflex action which may seem like they are acting hyperactive.

As you can see, this will cause difficulties when they face situations that fail to fully stimulate them, such as regular school work. Of cause, this can have a negative effect in the child's ability to be educated in the normal way.

Twenty years ago, there was not as much information about ADHD as we have today. A friend of mine who was a teacher twenty years ago, told me of a child who was in her class. This child would stand on his desk halfway through the class and tell jokes. At the time, the child was seen as disruptive and trying to seek attention. But as the years passed, it was discovered that he actually had ADHD. So he really would not have had much control over his actions.

In adult life, those with ADHD have difficulty trying to maintain personal relationships. They may also have problems with employment.

However, **it is getting easier as ADHD is more widely recognized and accepted.** But this does not necessarily mean that it is easy for those who have to carry this disorder.

Chapter 23: Stretch Your Attention Span

As an adult with ADHD, you are capable of focusing—it's just that you may have a hard time keeping that focus, especially when the activity isn't one that you find particularly engaging. Boring meetings or lectures are hard on anyone, but for adults with ADHD, they can be a special challenge. Similarly, following multiple directions can also be difficult for those with ADHD. Use these tips to improve your focus and ability to follow instructions:

Get it in writing if you're attending a meeting, lecture, workshop, or another gathering that requires close attention, ask for an advance copy of the relevant materials—such as a meeting agenda or lecture outline. At the meeting, use the written notes to guide your active listening and note taking. Writing as you listen will help you stay focused on the speaker's words.

Echo directions after someone gives verbal instructions, say them aloud to be sure you got it right.

Move around to prevent restlessness and fidgeting, go ahead and move around at the appropriate times in the right places. As long as you are not disturbing others, taking a walk or even jumping up and down during a meeting break, for example, can help you pay attention later on.

Exercise And Spend Time Outdoors

Working out is probably the most positive and efficient way to reduce hyperactivity and inattention from ADHD. Exercise can relieve stress, boost your mood, and calm your mind. Helping work off the excess energy and aggression that can get in the way of relationships and feeling stable.

Exercise on a daily basis. Choose something vigorous and fun that you can stick with, like a team sport or working out with a friend.

Increase stress relief by exercising outdoors. People with ADHD often benefit from sunshine and green surroundings.

Try relaxing forms of exercise, such as mindful walking, yoga, or tai chi. In addition to relieving stress, they can teach you to better control your attention and impulses.

Whatever your body can handle, is what you should be doing.

Get Plenty Of Sleep

Sleep deprivation can increase symptoms of adult ADHD, reducing your ability to cope with stress and maintain focus during the day. Simple changes to daytime habits go a long way toward ensuring solid nightly sleep.

Avoid caffeine late in the day.

Exercise vigorously and regularly, but not within an hour of bedtime.

Create a predictable and quiet "bedtime" routine, including taking a hot shower or bath just before bed.

Stick to a regular sleep-wake schedule, even on weekends.

It is extremely important to stick to a sleep schedule. If you go to sleep at 10pm on weeknights, you should go to bed at 10pm on the weekend. You should also wake up at the same time every single day.

Eat Right

While unhealthy eating habits don't cause ADHD, a poor diet can exacerbate symptoms. By making simple changes in what and how you eat, you may experience big reductions in distractibility, hyperactivity, and stress levels.

Eat small meals throughout day.

Avoid sugar and junk food as much as possible.

Make sure you include healthy protein at every meal.

Aim for several servings of fiber-rich whole grains each day.

Eating healthy will give you a giant mental boost. You will feel great and in turn focus better. There is no better feeling than eating healthy and exercising. Junk food makes our bodies slow and groggy. With the proper fuel, you will be able to keep you ADHD under control.

Do What You're Good At

Everyone is good at some things, and not so good at others. Often it's more productive to focus on improving your strengths rather than on trying to shore up your weak points.

And when you must do something you're not particularly good at? Work with family members, coaches, or tutors to find coping strategies that help you become "good enough."

With ADHD, you have probably become extremely good at something through hyper focus. Whatever that may be, continue to do it. Just make sure you always do it in moderation.

With these guidelines and some mental discipline. I am sure you can control your

ADHD and accomplish whatever it is you want to do.

Conclusion

ADHD is a genuine condition that adversely influences a kid's physical, mental, and social well-being. There are approaches to deal with ADHD and not every one of them includes the utilization of drugs. As a rule, ADHD is dealt with through prescriptions and behavioral strategies. However, looking for counsel from a specialist is imperative in light of the fact that appropriate determination and early treatment lessens the danger of any perpetual inconveniences.

Elective types of treatment include unwinding exercises that additionally enhance concentration, for example, yoga and meditation. Kids with ADHD will probably positively react to encouraging feedback strategies, for example, prizes and acclaim. Long term prizes are not as compelling, but rather combining short-term and long-term rewards has good results. Since ADHD once in a while results in poor scholarly execution, parents of kids with ADHD ought to consider other options to standard tutoring, for example, home schooling. On the other hand at any rate select a school that is equipped to manage ADHD.

There is no ideal strategy for dealing with ADHD. Converse with your specialist about the conceivable adapting systems and do not be reluctant to explore different avenues regarding diverse methods until you locate the ones which best suit you. When you do, stick to it. Consistency is vital. Adapting to ADHD is regularly a deep rooted attempt, yet with the correct mix of way of life changes and solutions, patients frequently live ordinary and productive lives.

Thank you and good luck!

www.ingramcontent.com/pod-product-compliance
Lightning Source LLC
Chambersburg PA
CBHW051720020426
42333CB00014B/1078